The British Bus Industry 1
BODYBUILDERS

THE BRITISH BUS INDUSTRY 1

BODYBUILDERS

Gavin Booth and Stewart J. Brown

LONDON

IAN ALLAN LTD

Previous page:

Different body styles on the same chassis can often look surprisingly different. These two Highland Omnibuses Albion Lowlanders date from the mid-1960s, and illustrate the differences. The bus on the right has Alexander bodywork, of a style that was carried by the first Lowlanders, a rather uneasy match of existing parts that produced a most uncomfortable appearance. Northern Counties, as seen by the bus on the left, managed to overcome the problems presented by a front-engined lowheight chassis, and produced a well-proportioned design. *SBG*

Front cover:

A painted and trimmed body on a Leyland Olympian chassis receives the final touches at Eastern Coach Works. *Leyland Bus*

First published 1987

ISBN 0 7110 1642 9

© Ian Allan Ltd 1987

Published by Ian Allan Ltd, Shepperton, Surrey; and printed by Ian Allan Printing Ltd at their works at Coombelands in Runnymede, England

Contents

Historical Perspective

You cannot easily ignore bus or coach bodies. Not only are they large and often brightly painted, they effectively hide the parts of the vehicle that make it go. Often all that is visible to confirm that there are mechanical units somewhere, is a set of wheels — and some bodybuilders would hide these too, if they were given a free hand.

Gone are the days when driver and passenger sat behind a prominent radiator and bonnet; gone, too, are the days when new rear-engined buses proclaimed the fact with a tail-end bustle. Since underfloor-engined single-deckers appeared on the scene, the bodybuilder has had almost total control of the look and layout of buses and coaches; and with the latest breed of rear-engined — and more particularly underfloor-engined — double-deckers, it is increasingly difficult to locate the engine at all. Four fleets in Scotland have similarly-bodied Volvo Ailsas (front-engined) and Citybuses (underfloor-engined), and it is sometimes difficult to tell them apart at first glance.

The coachbuilder's art was being practised many centuries before motorbuses appeared, by craftsmen in wood who produced a wide range of horse-drawn carriages. Although many of these were outwardly similar, their owners tended to demand individual features, and coachbuilders could accommodate their whims.

George Shillibeer, the man who in 1829 introduced the first regular horse-bus service in London, was himself a coachbuilder and undertaker — a logical combination for craftsmen in wood — and it was by no means rare to find coachbuilders dabbling in bus operation.

The growth of public transport in the 19th century created much work for coachbuilders, and encouraged the adoption of more efficient and standardised techniques. Carriages and wagons were required to satisfy the growing list of railway companies; horse-buses and trams were needed for the expanding industrial towns and cities.

The railway companies often built their own carriages and wagons, but specialist companies appeared to handle extra work, or supply the smaller railways. Some of these specialists also built horse-buses and trams, and moved on to electric tramcars and motorbuses.

As the market grew, the larger companies relied less on local coachbuilders, who now found themselves too small to tackle the work that was on offer. Local bus builders survived, though, and for many years were available to tackle repairs, and build small numbers of bus and coach bodies. Some survive to this day, but as construction methods have become more sophisticated,

Left:
Burlingham was using aluminium framing for these 1934 rear-entrance bodies on Leyland Tiger chassis for SMT; note the roof-mounted luggage rack and the 'Scottish' style cutaway rear entrance.
Gavin Booth (GB) collection

5

Right:
Panelling metal body sections for the SMT Tigers at Burlingham.
GB collection

Far right:
A Duple utility body of composite construction, to full restricted wartime specification; note the lack of opening windows, the square-cut rear dome and the lack of a window in the rear upstairs emergency exit. The grey livery disguises the fact that it was a Coventry Corporation bus, on Daimler CWG5 chassis.
Ian Allan Library (IAL)

bus and coach bodybuilding has become a more specialised craft.

In *Buses '71*, Alan Townsin colourfully described early bodybuilding as 'largely a matter of sending whatever chassis was chosen along to a firm of what could almost be described as high-class carpenters to knock-up a body for it, in much the same way as one would make some kitchen cupboards to suit an existing house'.

Although wood was most commonly used in early bus and tram building, many wooden bodies suffered badly from vibration on the poorly-surfaced roads of the time. Metal panels on wooden frames became more normal, and there were moves towards all-metal bodies. London General actually built an all-metal body on a B type before World War 1, but it would be the 1930s before all-metal bodies became a practical alternative.

With the development of new alloys in the 1920s, bus builders in the United States turned to alloy bodies around 1925, and these were general by 1940. But in Britain, Metropolitan-Cammell, with considerable railway experience, produced its first metal-framed bodies in 1929/30, Leyland followed in 1932 and Northern Counties and Park Royal in 1933. Leyland turned entirely to all-metal body production in 1934, but other builders continued to cater for customers requiring composite (wooden frame, metal panelling) construction.

During World War 2 builders were required to build composite bodies, with the wooden body framing forming the window pillars, and with steel external panels. Northern Counties was allowed to use steel framing and window pans, and its bodies often outlasted their utility brethren.

After the war most builders continued to produce both metal and composite bodies. The shortage of seasoned timber hastened the move towards metal construction, although most coach bodies were still wooden-framed. This was partly a consequence of the rash of new builders that flooded the postwar market, and the fact that smaller operators could handle wooden-framed body repairs more easily.

Some new coach bodies on underfloor-engined chassis were metal-framed, notably the Burlingham Seagull and Duple Road-master, but most contained wood until the late 1960s.

Glazing methods changed with the acceptance of direct rubber glazing in place of window pans; many of the lightweight bodies of the 1950s and 1960s achieved weight-saving and extra internal width with this style of window.

Some builders at this time started to experiment with glassfibre, which helped save weight, and allowed designers to achieve more adventurous shapes. Park Royal demonstrated how the entire roof above upper-deck waistrail level could be

Below:
Edinburgh Corporation's lightweight Leyland Titans of the mid-1950s had MCW Orion bodies and weighed little more than 6½ tons unladen. The lower saloon interior was basic, but practical, although several of the interior lining panels were omitted, and initially no opening windows were fitted. The Cronapress bell-strip was a new feature at the time. *MCW*

Right:
The AEC Regent V for Western Welsh which was displayed at the 1956 Commercial Motor Show had Park Royal bodywork featuring a completely detachable glassfibre roof. This early 30ft double-decker had a rear entrance with platform doors. *AEC*

Below right and far right:
Walter Alexander has constantly developed the use of glassfibre in its bodies, and produced one-piece mouldings for an entire lower saloon wheel-arch/seat base, and forward-ascending staircase.
Alexander

glassfibre on a Western Welsh AEC Regent V in 1956, but the most common uses were for the domes, front-end panels and roof centre panels. Gradually some builders developed entire wheel arch assemblies and staircases, and even entire glassfibre body framing; Eastern Coach Works built experimental bodies on Bristol SC chassis for Crosville and Eastern Counties.

As new materials have been developed, they have been adopted by bus bodybuilders. Bus and coach interiors have been improved with new laminates for roof and bulkhead panels and seat backs, new non-slip flooring surfaces, better and safer handrails and coverings. Interior lighting, initially acetylene, then electric tungsten bulbs, moved firmly to fluorescent tubes in the 1960s. Destination indicators, which first were fixed boards, and then became back-lit linen blinds, changed manually, have altered little, other than in shape and size — except for the expensive electronic displays, to be seen in some fleets, but by no means as widely as their makers might hope. For coach bodies, the adoption of bonded glazing, with windows fixed with adhesive, has allowed smoother lines, with less prominent window pillars.

Today, all-metal bodies are standard, but builders have their own preferred construction methods. Aluminium framing and body panels are used by bus builders like Alexander and Optare; all-steel structures are used by coachbuilders like Berkhof, Duple, Jonckheere, Mercedes-Benz and MCW (coaches only); and one-piece stretched steel side panels permit clean body lines, free of panel breaks. Increasingly, bodies are jig-built to exacting specifications for easy and precise assembly.

Representative of modern double-deck bus interiors, the upper deck of this London Buses Leyland Titan is bright and spacious, with hard-wearing seat moquette, non-slip floor covering, well-sited hand-holds, and discreet fluorescent lighting. The lower deck is dominated by the centre exit and centrally-placed stairs, but the design is thoroughly thought out, with low floors allowing 95% of Britons to stand upright — a greater proportion than is possible on most designs. *Leyland*

Operator Influence

Bus bodies inevitably reflect the requirements of their proud owners, but perhaps to a lesser degree than might be thought. Operators have always had a certain amount of freedom in specifying such items as seats (how many? what kind? moquette or not?), the interior colour scheme, the type and number of opening windows or ventilators, the destination indicator layout — but the overall appearance of the bus, good or bad, has frequently been under the control of the bodybuilder, with only an attractive livery to disguise what has often been a very bland appearance.

Obviously, commercial considerations play their part. An independent bus operator buying one new double-deck bus each year can hardly insist that the bodybuilder produces it to a unique design; often he is forced to take a run-on from a batch for a major customer, and so individuality must be sacrificed for economy. But there have been times when bodybuilders have seemed hell-bent on giving the customer what they, the bodybuilders, deemed most appropriate, with arguments of economies of scale, advantages of standardisation and common parts.

Sometimes these arguments make sense, particularly in the case of chassis-less integral buses produced on an assembly-line basis. A Leyland National is a Leyland National, whether you are AA of Ayr or London Transport — the individuality of the operators is expressed in the livery and interior trim. Likewise Leyland Titans and MCW Metrobuses were devised as highly-standardised vehicles with large orders and easy replacement of parts as important considerations.

The Titan and Metrobus were designed with London Transport firmly in mind. As Britain's biggest bus operator, with requirements for literally hundreds of buses each year, manufacturers would be foolish to ignore London's needs. And right from the earliest days of the motorbus, London's needs have influenced bus design and, consequently, the manufacturers.

London's early buses were subject to the whims of the Metropolitan Police, as the vehicle licensing authority, and trend-setting designs like the famous London B type of 1910 were designed to meet the exacting requirements of the Police. With an eye to London orders, other manufacturers produced similar buses, and these appeared throughout Britain as the motorbus grew more popular.

The restrictive nature of many of the London regulations meant that Londoners missed out on refinements like pneumatic tyres and covered-top double-deckers for some time after passengers in the rest of the country had enjoyed them. By the mid-1920s, though, manufacturers were finding their feet, and important designs like the Leyland PLSC Lion of 1925 came with a Leyland-designed standard body, built by Leyland and other builders. Leyland further influenced bus design with the Titan TD1 double-decker of 1927, which pioneered a shape and a general layout that lasted for some 40 years.

By the 1930s some of the major operators and operating groups were seeking to express their individuality by commissioning special bus and coach designs from bodybuilders. London had been doing this from 1910, but in the 1920s and 1930s there emerged a distinctive London look that was not taken up by other operators.

Many municipal transport systems only really started to buy motorbuses in large numbers in the 1930s, having previously been principally tramway operators, and the major cities expressed their civic pride, and exercised their buying power with bodybuilders, by specifying distinctive bus designs. Birmingham Corporation devised a handsome, restrained design with luxurious interior fittings, which lasted in production, with variations, for 20 years. Manchester Corporation opted for a more flamboyant approach, with downswept windows to give a fashionable streamline look; this design too emerged in a modified form in the postwar period.

While the Birmingham and Manchester designs were clearly 'specials', other big city fleets took what were basically standard body

Left:

Independents requiring new double-deckers often have to accept a vehicle built to the specification of a larger customer. Cunningham's of Paisley took this West Yorkshire PTE-style Roe-bodied Leyland Atlantean for this reason.
Stewart J. Brown (SJB)

Below left:

A Hants & Dorset Bristol K5G with ECW body. This is a typical Tilling bus of the late 1930s — actually a 1940 delivery, hence the wartime livery. *M. J. Tozer collection*

Below:

The Alexander body design on a Leyland TS8 special was the ultimate prewar development of a range of bodies for SMT group companies. This example for the Alexander's fleet, lasted more than 20 years in service. *GB*

Above:

Roe's first bodies for rear-engined double-deckers were disappointingly bland, like this Tynemouth Leyland Atlantean with offside illuminated advert panel, a short-lived fashion. *GB*

Above right:

Liverpool's MCW-bodied Atlanteans reintroduced municipal individuality, and prompted operators and coachbuilders to look hard at the designs for their new buses. *GB*

Above right and right:

Although the ECW body for the Bristol RELL was frequently facelifted, the basic, sound body lines were largely unchanged. The Lincolnshire example shows the early front end, with curved-glass screens, and a rather ungainly destination layout. The later example, in Badgerline's distinctive yellow and green livery, shows the final version with BET-style screen. *C. W. Routh; SJB*

designs with individual touches that immediately distinguished them.

The growth of the big company fleet groupings in the 1930s meant that BET, Tilling, SMT and their offshoots emerged as important customers for bus and coach bodies. Conscious of their buying power, the groups evolved their own designs, usually single-deck buses, and while some of the member companies took these, others continued to go their own way, and there was no apparent compulsion to toe the party line.

The BET group had formed a central purchasing organisation in 1907, British Electrical Federation Ltd, and in the early 1930s an instantly recognisable BEF style emerged; the design was built by various major builders, notably Brush, ECW, Roe and Weymann, and although similar, they were by no means identical. Double-deck purchases by BET fleets tended to stick to standard manufacturers' designs.

The Tilling group had its own in-group manufacturing facilities: chassis by Bristol, and bodies by Eastern Counties. The Bristol Tramways operating company had built chassis since its earliest days, and these were sold commercially to other operators. United had set up its own bodybuilding factory at Lowestoft, which passed to Eastern Counties when reorganisation of operations took place in 1931. Tilling decided to concentrate most of the group's vehicle manufacturing at Bristol and Eastern Counties, and by 1934 many Tilling fleets were taking deliveries. In 1936 the Lowestoft factory became Eastern Coach Works, and ECW continued to supply Tilling fleets, and also sought outside work including contracts for BET fleets. By the outbreak of war in 1939 the Bristol/ECW combination was fast becoming the Tilling standard.

In Scotland, the SMT group had its own in-group bodybuilders, Alexander, an offshoot of the operating company. Although Alexander had undertaken some outside work, most of its production had been for its own use; with its new links with the SMT companies, most of its output was for group fleets in the 1930s, but the group's vehicle requirements were so great that other bodybuilders were used. Alexander produced a small range of adaptable designs, and created a look as distinctive as that on BET and Tilling buses. It concentrated on single-deck vehicles until the war.

Operators' whims were fast forgotten when war broke out in 1939. Buses continued to be built to prewar standards for a short time until all production was frozen in 1941. When in 1942 the vehicles in production were unfrozen, they were allocated to fleets throughout Britain on an apparently random basis, which meant that individualistic operators received 'ordinary' buses, and 'ordinary' operators were given buses that had clearly been destined elsewhere. With the development of a standard utility specification for new buses, individuality disappeared totally, and operators large and small, depending on their needs, received identical buses.

After the war individuality and standardisation were sacrificed for new deliveries; operators took literally anything they could, and fleets like London Transport and Birmingham Corporation were forced to take deliveries of highly-standardised early postwar designs in the interests of expediency.

Once the situation had settled down, operators sought to return to the prewar standards, but found bodybuilders less prepared to accommodate them. London Transport's 'clout' was still enough to make sure that the RT family could be produced on a highly-standardised jig-built basis by four different builders. But other operators seemed prepared to compromise, and accepted adaptations of standard bodybuilders' designs.

Obvious BET designs were less apparent, although BET was heavily involved in discussions with major builders in the planning stages of new bodies, and the group's influence was very strong. Park Royal, for example, decided in the mid-1950s to change from aluminium alloy construction to steel framing, to suit BET.

The nationalisation of the Tilling and SMT groups in 1948/49 affected their in-house bodybuilders. Bristol and ECW, now nationalised, could only build for other nationalised fleets — principally Tilling, SMT and London Transport. In practice, Tilling fleets bought Bristol/ECW products until the mid-1960s; SMT, now the Scottish Bus Group, bought Bristol/ECW products and anything else it chose; and London Transport largely stuck to its established suppliers, except for some ECW bodies.

When SMT was nationalised, the Alexander coachworks remained in the family's hands, and was increasingly able to accept outside work in addition to the firm base of SBG work, which included several batches on Bristol chassis. As principal customer, SBG

The square-cut lines of the trend-setting Manchester Corporation Mancunian design, on a Fleetline, were seen in use at Caernarvon on the day of the Investiture of the Prince of Wales in 1969. The application of the Manchester red and cream livery adds to the overall effect. Ralph Bennett, Manchester's General Manager, was involved in developing this design, and had previously been general manager at Bolton Corporation. Designs like the East Lancs-bodied Atlantean of 1966 shown here were clearly moving in the same direction.
SJB; T. W. Moore

Right:
The Park Royal bodywork for Sheffield helped set a standard for many builders in the 1970s, particularly with regard to pillar spacing. This was a 10m Leyland Atlantean in Sheffield's attractive white and dark blue colours. *SJB*

influence was strong in many Alexander bodies, particularly for single-deck vehicles.

Weight-saving and standardisation were two of the preoccupations of the 1950s, and the result was a dreary succession of bland body styles from builders that had excellent pedigrees. The first bodies on the rear-engined double-deckers in the late 1950s were disappointingly unimaginative, and it seemed that most of the major builders had lost their feel for design. It took a rebirth of municipal pride to spur the builders into fresh action, and a refreshing new series of individual designs appeared that came to terms with the inevitable boxiness of the rear-engined buses. Liverpool and Glasgow were the first municipalities to influence dramatic new styles, and in a few years nearly every major municipality had returned to the days of individuality.

Several technical innovations and legislative changes helped the process: better curved glass windscreens were possible when opening windscreens were no longer needed for bus drivers; new glass-fibre techniques allowed imaginative curves; and relaxation of length and width regulations removed many restrictions, and presented new challenges.

The 11m (36ft) single-deck bus, legalised in 1961, prompted a new BET-influenced design that lasted on the market for many years. Built by most of the major firms, it featured attractive front and rear curved windscreens, and domes with a slight peak. Alexander produced the famous Y-type body in 1961, a style that remained in production for over 20 years. Tilling's 11m single-decker was the Bristol RE, and although the bodywork had a distinctive ECW look, it was competent and attractive, and, with variations, remained in production until the mid-1970s.

The operators with the greatest influence on vehicle design and layout were those with the closest links to the builders. New designs from Bristol/ECW — and there were very few of these — were considered by Tilling group committees. London Transport had designed its trolleybus-replacement bus, the Route-master, in production from 1959 at AEC and Park Royal. Midland Red, with a history of own-make buses dating back to the 1920s, continued to design and build most of the vehicles required for its large fleet, and pioneered several features and techniques that later became widely accepted.

The creation of the first Passenger Transport Executives in 1969/70 prompted these super-authorities to develop new standard vehicles to replace the varied mixture they had inherited from their municipal constituents. SELNEC PTE, operating in the Manchester conurbation, inherited not only the most mixed fleet, but also a tradition of producing technically and aesthetically advanced buses. The 1968 Mancunian design of Manchester Corporation was the first purpose-built one-man operated double-decker, and in 1972 it was refined to appear as a new standard design. The other PTEs, Merseyside, Tyneside and West Midlands, also expressed their new identities in standard designs, though less dramatically than SELNEC.

Most operators benefited from the fresh interest being shown in body design. A 1968 Park Royal design for Sheffield Corporation became the basis for a most acceptable double-deck style, adopted by other builders as, almost, an industry standard. Not all builders followed — Alexander, East Lancs and ECW all stuck to existing ideas on pillar-spacing.

Above and Above right:
Nottingham City Transport earned a reputation for having individual ideas on body design and layout, resulting in some unusual confections. Earlier versions are represented by No 526, a 1970 Northern Counties-bodied Leyland Atlantean, while No 398 is a 1983 Volvo Citybus with East Lancs body.
Alan D. Broughall; SJB

The later PTEs, Greater Glasgow, South Yorkshire and West Yorkshire, developed body styles of their own, based on builders' standard designs; Glasgow and West Yorkshire achieved this fairly quickly, while South Yorkshire's recent Dennis Dominators were perhaps the PTE's first large-scale standard.

The Leyland National changed the rules when it appeared in 1970. There was initially very little element of choice, for here was a bus assembled on a production line, like a private car, with little room for individuality. Leyland's initial hard line on choices softened a bit, and operators had some leeway, but the National anticipated not only a wider acceptance of integral construction, but also a move towards greater standardisation.

Bristol and ECW products returned to the open market in 1965, and this meant initially that Tilling-like buses appeared in other fleets. Then in 1968 Tilling's owner, the Transport Holding Co, acquired the BET companies, leading to the formation of the National Bus Co (NBC) in 1969. NBC had a Tilling-like view of standardisation, with two principal bus models, the Leyland National

single-deck and Bristol/ECW VRT double-deck, and although this was not observed as religiously as in Tilling days, there were few major changes to this pattern from the mid-1970s. Added to this, NBC's decision to paint its service buses either poppy red or leaf green only emphasised the standardisation. More recently, greater individuality has been apparent in NBC fleets, both in vehicle policy and livery application, and this has been undoubtedly a prelude to privatisation.

Most of the larger municipalities disappeared into the PTEs, and few of the remaining fleets were big enough to express their individuality. The biggest, Edinburgh and Nottingham, came up with distinctive styles — Edinburgh's a development of standard designs, Nottingham's a decidely nonconformist style that has remained unique.

London Transport's post-Routemaster track record has been less impressive. The experimental Atlanteans and Fleetlines of 1966 were hardly inspiring; the large fleet of AEC Merlins and Swifts had bodies that were unique to London, but fairly bland; and the DMS class Fleetlines from 1970 onwards were possibly the least inspired variant of the Park Royal industry standard. Only the Metrobus and Titan models have been successful, and these are manufacturers' designs, albeit with strong London influence. London was working in the background on a new model, the XRM, and drawings suggest that this might have marked a return to London's normally high standards, had it not been aborted. Recent work for London Buses by Ogle, with particular attention to the front end and entrance area, suggest that we may soon see London as trend-setters once again.

Leyland National

In the mid-1960s Leyland and the Transport Holding Co (THC) started to talk about a standard single-deck bus. The THC fleets had a respected single-deck model, the Bristol RELL, built only for nationalised fleets, like all Bristol/ECW products since nationalisation in 1948. A 1965 share exchange between Bristol and Leyland removed this restriction, and allowed other operators to buy Bristols, which they readily did. The Leyland group already had three rear-engined single-deck models, the AEC Swift, Leyland Panther and Leyland Panther Cub, but none of these chassis could be described as an unqualified success.

During the 1960s several large operators had turned to single-deckers to save money by speeding the spread of one-man operation (OMO). Double-deck OMO was not possible at the time, so high-capacity single-deckers were appearing in some unlikely places, including such cities as Glasgow, Leeds, Liverpool, London and Manchester.

In 1968 British Leyland was formed, and added to the rear-engined single-deck family was the unhappy Daimler Roadliner chassis. There was an obvious need for rationalisation, and the new BL, together with the new NBC, formed the Leyland National Co Ltd to design, produce and market a new standardised single-deck citybus to replace its mixed inheritance; NBC was the successor to the Transport Holding Co.

The result of their liaison, the Leyland National, was shown to the world in 1970. It was a highly-standardised integral bus, which would be produced using methods new to the bus industry. A new factory was built at Workington, and production lines similar

to those used for private cars were installed. None of the traditional chassis-building and body-building techniques were employed, for Workington was conceived as an assembly plant, largely using unskilled labour.

The level of standardisation shocked many in the industry, used to tailoring buses to suit their own needs. The National was available in just two lengths, 10.3m and 11.3m, with one or two doors, and in right-hand or left-hand drive form. Up to 40 of these buses could be produced in a week, though in practice only 20 emerged in the best weeks because orders never reached the anticipated levels. But even at this rate, the National was a big seller, and while Leyland was undoubtedly happy to have simplified its range, the bodybuilders who had previously built on Leyland group single-deck bus chassis were less so.

Operators bought the bus in spite of their criticisms about lack of choice, and Leyland may have underestimated their desire for individuality. Buses were initially only available in red, green or white — a 1970s version of Henry Ford's famous utterance 'Any colour, so long as it's black' — although eventually other colours and more complex liveries could be accommodated; in practice, many operators took Nationals in one-colour

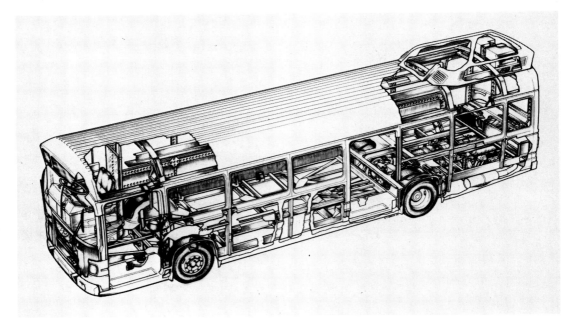

Above:
A cut-away elevation of the National, showing the ring-frame structure integrated with the underframe to ensure low floor levels. *Leyland*

schemes and added relief colours after delivery.

As if to confound its critics, Leyland started to offer National variants. There was a dual-purpose version, with coach seats, and there were mobile banks, prison vehicles, luxury commuter versions, and even an in-between-length 10.9m version for the Australian market.

The benefits of the thorough research that went into the National certainly paid off. Production settled down from an early stage, and structurally the bus has presented few problems; operators have found parts standardisation a boon when repairing accident damage.

Of course the National has had its critics, but in many cases these were of the mechanical content: the 500 engine originally fitted was not popular with all operators, and the 680 unit in the 1979 Mk 2 version proved uncharacteristically troublesome. However, the body, with its wide, low front entrance and interior floor, has made travel much easier for thousands of people, and the structural rigidity has saved injury in accidents. The only real criticism of the body has been its almost clinical interior trim, considerably less welcoming than many contemporary vehicles, although undoubtedly easy to maintain. Criticisms that the National's sophistication rendered it unsuitable for rural duties prompted the B series in 1978, a simpler specification without the distinctive roof-mounted pod containing the heating/ventilating system.

The only significant change to the appearance of the National was the revised frontal structure to house the front-mounted radiator of the 1979 Mk 2 version, and the consequent changes to the rear. The main body structure remained unchanged; and, although further options were offered, when production ceased in 1985 after nearly 8,000 vehicles, the body concept was the same as it had been in 1970. Its successor, the Lynx, was designed as an underframe capable of carrying bodywork built other than at Workington; one of the reasons for the National's non-acceptance in some overseas markets had been the lack of local content in the bodywork, an important political consideration in many countries.

But the National technology was not dead. Leyland had diversified into railbus production, using a high proportion of National bus parts, and this enterprising development was rewarded with orders from British Rail. The first production National Railbuses entered service in 1984 for use in the West Yorkshire PTE area and subsequent deliveries have been for Greater Manchester and for BR provincial services.

Top:
The National body structure from the inside, looking to the rear. *Leyland*

Above:
National bodies were assembled separately from the running units, and at this stage were matched. *Leyland*

Above:
London Country built up a large National fleet, including batches of these B series buses, shorter-length vehicles distinguished by the absence of the roof-pods. *SJB*

Left:
Apart from the longer snout and changes to the rear, the National 2 was clearly derived from the original version. A late-model National 2 from the fleet of McGill, Barrhead. *SJB*

Below left:
National interiors were clean and simple. *GB*

Above right, centre and below:
Liveries could affect the appearance of the National. Although many have been in NBC red or green, some subsequently wore less straightforward schemes like this example in Alder Valley local coach livery, red, black and white. Lothian's 11.6m National 2s featured an attractive layout in madder and white. Contrast the Portsmouth bus — similar colours, different layout.
SJB, Ian M. Train, Leyland

Selling their Wares

Bus and coach bodybuilders have always used the pages of the trade press to publicise their products. When competition has been at its greatest, so has the level of advertising. Around 1950 the monthly magazine *Bus and Coach* might have around 30 coachbuilders advertising in its pages, but when the competition reduced, it was usually left to the luxury coachbuilders — Burlingham, Duple, Harrington, Plaxton; the bus bodybuilders did not really need to advertise, and only the biggest did. MCW and Park Royal-Roe advertised regularly; Alexander only did at Motor Show times; ECW, East Lancs and Northern Counties rarely if ever did.

With the formation of British Leyland in 1968 the previous range of adverts from BLMC constituents was reduced considerably. Only with the increase in competition from continental bodybuilders did British builders resume advertising at previous levels.

Graphic design has usually been a secondary consideration. The bus and coach business has always relied on simply-designed adverts with prominent illustrations. Clever design and copywriting has rarely found favour; more acceptable is a photograph of a sparkling coach in brilliant sunshine — usually with no passengers — against an unlikely background. Even worse is the artist's impression, a fanciful illustration that often gives the impression that the coach is roughly twice its real length.

There have been exceptions, of course. This accompanying illustrative selection shows some bodybuilders' adverts, good and bad, from the past half-century.

Above:
A simple, but effective, 1935 advertisement for English Electric, all the type matter hand- lettered in these far-off days before Letraset. English Electric did not return to bus bodybuilding after World War 2.

Below:
Duple was one of Britain's most successful bodybuilders in the 1930s, and many bodies were built on Bedford chassis. This 1936 advert for the Vista coach used stock typefaces, with a hand-drawn, non-standard logo.

Bottom left:
Many of the advertisements around 1950 did little more than feature the company name and a front three-quarter view of a recent coach. Windovers had the added selling points of a Royal Warrant and a long history. The main part of the advert was hand-lettered.

Bottom right:
Yeates enjoyed a brief success in the 1950s, building heavily-ornamented coaches at Loughborough, and doubtless felt that its advertising had to be in keeping with its products. This is a hand-lettered ad from 1953.

EVERY SEAT
– a Window Seat

EVERY SEAT
– a "Super" Seat

EVERY SEAT
– with Visibility

A "VISTA" Coach
built by Duple on Bedford Chassis offers these 1937 features.

● *For Coachwork Details apply to —*
Scottish Motor Traction Co. Ltd., Roseburn St., Edinburgh ; or direct to DUPLE BODIES.

DUPLE BODIES & MOTORS LTD.
Edgware Road, The Hyde, Hendon, LONDON, N.W. 9
Telephone : COLINDALE 6412 (Private Exchange)   Cables : "DUPLE, HENDON LONDON"
Telegrams : "DUPLE, HYDE, HENDON"   Codes : BENTLEY'S, ABC (6th Edition)

WINDOVERS LIMITED

BY APPOINTMENT TO HIS MAJESTY THE KING, COACHBUILDERS

COACHWORK SPECIALISTS
SINCE 1796

The "Huntingdon"
The Windover Body, supplied to the order of Sheffield United Tours, on A.E.C. Chassis which was awarded first prize in the International Coach Rally at Montreux in June.

THE HYDE, HENDON. LONDON. N.W.9
TELEPHONE COLINDALE 4031-2-3-4

Yeates
GRACEFUL CONTOUR COACHWORK

RIVIERA

So great is the demand for our 'Riviera' luxury coach that we earnestly ask operators to let us know their requirements now.
Our 'Riviera' 41-seater luxury touring coach is available in light-weight form for the A.E.C. Reliance chassis.

W. S. YEATES LTD., DERBY RD., LOUGHBOROUGH.
PASSENGER VEHICLE SPECIALISTS   Phone: LOUGHBOROUGH 4321 (4 lines).

YEATES

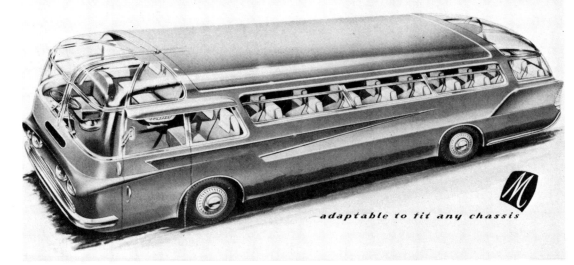

adaptable to fit any chassis

Above and right:
Mulliners attempted to break into the coach body market with a design that was nothing if not dramatic. It was not quite as startling as the artist's impression might suggest, but certainly different as the photograph of the real thing confirms.

Facing page, top left:
Park Royal-Roe's advertising was straightforward, rarely exciting; the photograph, the name, the logos, the address. Only the vehicles changed — this was a Northern General Routemaster in a 1965 ad.

Facing page, top right:
Rivals MCW had a more adventurous approach to advertising, and ran a series of these Photo Call ads in the 1960s. This 1965 one featured a Bournemouth Leyland Atlantean/Weymann, a design cribbed from the contemporary Alexander style.

Facing page, bottom left:
Plaxtons' advertising was normally staid and straightforward, but it temporarily tried a more modern approach with this 1966 Panorama advert.

Facing page, bottom right:
MCW's earlier forays into the luxury coach body business were largely unsuccessful: perhaps the company's unconventional advertising did not appeal to traditional coach customers. This 1968 ad for the Metropolitan was decidedly outspoken for the time — it actually mentioned the price!

Putting on the Style

The Burlingham Seagull and Harrington Cavalier had it; the MCW Orion and early Caetano coaches did not. The Setra range has it; the Alexander P type does not. Style, like beauty, is in the eye of the beholder, but what dictates style? Of course if there was a single answer, designers could relax, perhaps retire. But style reflects public taste, which is constantly changing, and to a degree creates public taste.

In the 1920s coaches were based largely on service bus body designs, with the luxury effect confined to the interior — veneered wood, curtains, comfortable moquette-covered seats, clocks. But coachbuilders had a traditional feel for balanced design and produced easy-on-the-eye coaches, not dramatic and flashy, but undeniably solid and handsome.

Then with the 1930s came a general atmosphere of fresh hope, often expressed in a reaction against tradition, and a ready acceptance of anything obviously new; there was an awareness of streamlining, both in terms of its aesthetic appeal and its wind-resistant properties, so motor cars, trains and aeroplanes all appeared in streamlined guise. Motor coaches too were affected, for coachbuilders were coming to terms with shaping metal, and designers experimented with the new shapes. Builders and operators assumed that the public expected streamlined coaches, and so these were produced; they were not always successful, but they pushed

back the frontiers and paved the way for later, and more attractive, designs.

Most coaches had their engines at the front, so a streamlined full-width front was one way of modernising the appearance. There was an aerodynamic advantage, but with a 30mph speed limit this was hardly a consideration. There were even some attempts at streamlined double-deckers, without much success, but these did lead to cleaner lines. Attempts by Roe and London Transport in the late 1930s produced sleeker designs that anticipated later standards.

The appearance of models like the AEC Q and Maudslay SF40 in the 1930s, which allowed 'proper' full fronts and front entrances ahead of the axle, gave designers a greater opportunity to move forward, and some most attractive buses and coaches appeared.

Style was not really a consideration during World War 2, but in spite of the severe limitations imposed on builders when the utility specification appeared, some designers were able to produce buses that were well-proportioned, even handsome, and looked right for the job.

Postwar style owed much to prewar style while the bus industry geared up for a return to normal. With longer single-deck buses and coaches from 1950, many on underfloor-engined chassis, the bodybuilders had a field-day producing designs that covered the entire range between the sublime and the ridiculous. Those with style recognised the potential offered by new shapes and chassis layouts, but also understood the need for subtlety rather than ostentation; one of the most admired coach bodies of the time, by ECW on the Bristol LS, was a masterpiece of understatement.

As mentioned in the chapter on 'Operator Influence', operators and builders in the 1950s were obsessed by weight-saving, and in adopting new and simpler methods of construction they succeeded in producing bodies that were often singularly lacking in style. On service buses, the return to style was influenced considerably by the operators; but with only a handful of firms left building

Far left:
Flamboyant but hardly stylish. This Ford R226 had one of the very first Salvador Caetano bodies imported into Britain from Portugal, in 1967. *Ford*

Left:
One of the most stylish and widely admired coach bodies of the 1960s was the Harrington Cavalier; this early example is on an AEC Reliance for Northern General. *GB*

Below left:
Practical but with no concessions to style, the Alexander P-type bus body replaced the long-running Y-type, but lacked its good looks. This Northern Scottish P-type was on a Leyland Tiger; the similarly-bodied Dennis Lancets in the same fleet were higher-built, and consequently even more ungainly. *SJB*

Chassis like the AEC Q gave coachbuilders an early opportunity to experiment with body design. This side-engined AEC Q of 1934, for Silver Service of Darley Dale, had a Willowbrook centre-entrance body well-suited to the dimensions of the vehicle, and with an admirable lack of unnecessary brightwork.
IAL

luxury coaches, there was great competition to secure business by facelifts and innovation. Plaxtons, emerging as a major force to rival Burlingham, Duple and Harrington, won the race in 1958 with the Panorama body, the start of a trend to big windows that even spread to double-deckers. Bigger windows left less metal to be embellished, and encouraged operators to buy simpler, less flashy coaches than had previously been seen; as with contemporary private cars, excessive brightwork was equated with popular taste.

Many bus and coach bodies are evolutionary, and their development can be traced over a number of years, through successive designs. The first Plaxton Panorama was an existing design with big windows, and subsequent models tended to retain some features of their predecessors.

Leyland started with a clean sheet with the design for the National single-deck bus, familiar today, but decidely different when first seen in 1970. It owed little to previous designs, with its wedge-edge roof, pronounced window pillars, sculpted side mouldings and roof-mounted pod. Perhaps more practical than pretty, the National had undoubted style, and has influenced subsequent single-deck buses from other builders.

The '1970s standard' double-deck body style, built by several firms, evolved through designs built for different operators; its main 'difference' was the side window pillar spacing, which helped the body to sit happily on rear-engined designs. Not all builders adopted this spacing, and stuck to pillar spacing that was developed for front-engined models. More recently, the arrival of the 'new generation' double-deck models, some with

Left:
The Eastern Coach Works body on the Bristol LS was a solid, simply-styled design that resisted the ostentation of many of its contemporaries. Most were in a predominantly cream livery, with company colours restricted to window surrounds and mudwings. A Scottish Omnibuses 1954 example is illustrated. *GB*

Below left:
The Plaxtons Panorama was an important trend-setter; this early example, on a Leyland Tiger Cub chassis, was in the fleet of Wilkinsons of Sedgefield. *SJB*

Below:
Plaxtons also led the way with the Elite body range, featuring big, gently curving side windows. This is an Elite II on an AEC Reliance chassis for Glenton Tours. *AEC*

Right:
Duple followed Plaxtons with the similar Dominant in 1972, although this was a late-model Dominant II, with deeper front windscreen, on a Leyland Tiger for Midland Scottish. *SJB*

Below right:
ECW developed a coach body in a similar mould to the Dominant, here on a Bristol RELH chassis for Northern General in an attractive pre-NBC livery. *NGT*

Below:
The Willowbrook 003 body, supplied in quantity to NBC fleets, was visually similar to the Duple Dominant I; this Cambus Leyland Leopard was in National Express livery. *SJB*

box-frame chassis complete with outriggers that influence pillar spacing, has produced a new standard; although there is now a greater similarity between the products of the few remaining double-deck bodybuilders, they retain their individuality in many ways, and recognition is easier now than it was in the 1970s.

During the early 1970s there was little choice in the luxury coach body market. Only Duple and Plaxton were producing in quantity, and designs were becoming stunted. Plaxton's Panorama had become the Elite, with big curved side windows, and Duple had produced a similar design, the Dominant. These competent if unexciting products were all that were available to British operators until a trickle of imported coach bodies from Europe turned into a steady stream. The Continental designs were crisp and square-cut, and the British designs looked outdated and lacked style by comparison. When deregulation of express services heralded the coaching boom in 1980, operators looking for distinctive up-market vehicles often turned to the Continentals. Duple and Plaxton tried to facelift their models with features like smaller windows, but this could only be a stop-gap exercise. Smaller windows were becoming more familiar at the time, partly as a result of EEC doubts about the structural safety of coaches.

Duple and Plaxton each introduced new coach ranges in 1982, and although they were designed to meet the Continental challenge, they retain a distinctively British style which distinguishes them from some of the Continental designs, which tend to become indistinguishable. Other new British designs in 1982 were the MCW Metroliner, very much in the European mould, and the Leyland Royal Tiger Doyen, a boldly-styled integral.

Stylish, but in a more bizarre way, was the Neoplan Skyliner, the first three-axle double-deck coach to appear in Britain. Its competitors have been more predictable, but are nonetheless impressive.

Minibuses, on the other hand, are not meant to be impressive, but sadly they are not stylish either. Certainly the familiar box-like van conversions offer little scope. The midibus, however, offers greater scope, and Bedford demonstrated in 1976 with the JJL that a small bus could be stylish. Although the project was dropped, it has a worthy successor in the Dennis Domino, particularly as bodied by Northern Counties for Greater Manchester.

Below:
Plaxtons responded to fashion with the small-windowed Supreme VI, hardly the most stylish body of recent years. This one was on an early Leyland Tiger, for Rhondda-based Thomas Coaches. *Leyland*

Above:
A British response to imported rear-engined integral coaches like the German Setra, this Leyland Royal Tiger Doyen is in National Holidays livery. *Leyland*

Below:
This current midibus design was developed by Northern Counties for Greater Manchester PTE on the Dennis Domino rear-engined chassis. *SJB*

Sellar's Market

There has long been a suspicion among observers of the bus industry that bus and coach bodies are designed by competent, if unimaginative, staff whose principal concerns are structural rigidity and use of common parts, with little attention paid to external appearance. Certainly there have been many bus bodies that seemed to bear this out.

And there is the argument that buses do not *need* to look good; they are, after all, workaday machines, and a passenger at a bus stop at 06.30 on a wet winter's morning is hardly going to be influenced by the *look* of the vehicle. This view, not unreasonable in itself, underestimates the intelligence and design-awareness of the passenger. Millions of pounds are spent by the car giants trying to achieve appearances that are both practical and attractive; if the bus has to compete with the private car, many operators argue that it must look equally attractive and welcoming, and stand as an attractive part of the street scene.

The greater interest shown in bus and coach design standards has been partly prompted by awareness of the value of good design in the environment — but no doubt also by the increasing competition for reducing orders. This has been particularly noticeable among the coachbuilders, where competition from mainland Europe has prompted crisper designs.

Although often the basic body design may be an in-house product, builders are turning increasingly to styling consultants to advise on the finished appearance, or to facelift existing bodies. A designer who has been involved in this type of work is Dawson Sellar, working from Dundrennan, in south-west Scotland. Sellar was responsible for the reworking of the Alexander T type service coach body as a full luxury coach, and the distinctive RDC double-deck coach for the same builder.

Sellar studied industrial design on a four-year course at the Royal College of Art, in London, followed by a two-year transportation course, sponsored by Ford, and then moved to Ford at Dagenham as a staff designer. After two years he went to West Germany, where he joined the Porsche design team. In 1977 he moved to BMW, where he worked on cars and later motorcycles, but in 1980 he returned to Britain, looking for work in the domestic car industry.

He set up as an industrial design and styling consultant in his native Scotland, and

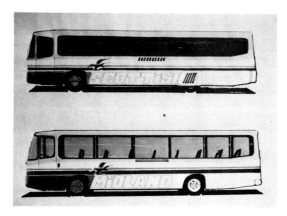

Above:
Two of Sellar's original styling sketches for the TC coach design, which included livery suggestions and, on one, enclosed rear wheels.

Above:
Neat interior styling ideas for the TC type that were never carried out.

Right:
An early design sketch for the RDC type double-deck coach body.

Below right:
Sellar's restyled front-end structure for the Alexander P-type bus body.

Bottom:
Coachbuilders are paying increasing attention to aerodynamics, and this scale model of Duple's 425 Integral was built to test wind resistance.

Facing page, top:
The first Class 143 railbus, built by Alexander and with Sellar styling on the front end and interior.

Facing page, bottom:
The end result — the first Alexander RDC body, for Fife Scottish, on Volvo Citybus chassis. Note the clever use of standard windscreens.

his first contact with larger commercial vehicles was with the Irvine-based fire engine builder, Fulton & Wylie. Sellar acknowledges the help of the Design Council in Glasgow in securing this work, which was handled on a funded consultancy basis, a scheme sponsored by the Department of Trade & Industry to encourage the wider use of specialist skills.

Among the firms he approached was Walter Alexander, the Falkirk bus and coach-builder, and the result of a 15-day funded project was the facelift for the T type body, which emerged in 1983 as the TC type.

The T type had first appeared as a service coach for 11m underfloor-engined chassis in

1974, a design with potential, but perhaps let down by the awkward front end, which was unreservedly bus-like. In 1983 Walter Alexander had replaced the basic T type with the TE type, a design that improved the front end by eliminating the awkward roofline step, and placing the destination indicator inside a deeper front windscreen.

Sellar's brief was to restyle the TE type as a 'proper' coach. But while designers would prefer to start from scratch, in practice there were many constraints. The pillar spacing and general outline of the body could not be changed; the existing windscreen had to be used. Working within these restrictions he changed from gasket to bonded glazing,

WALTER ALEXANDER'S NEW RANGE OF COACHES

Artist's Pre-release Impression

The new 'TE' type Coach. Available for 1983 season and the likely ch
for the rest of the 80's.
All Light Aluminium Alloy structure, combining with elegance, hig
specification and realistic pricing to set the top standard from
January 1983 and beyond.

When Alexander introduced the T type body in 1974, it was intended as an 11m dual-purpose vehicle, of the type beloved of SBG fleets. Although the body framing was new, the front end was bus-like, and not unlike the existing T type (*top left*) (this example is an Eastern Scottish Seddon Pennine). In 1982 the TE range was announced, with a restyled front and rear end — although perhaps better looking than the artist's impression released at the time (*left*). The restyling was effective, and produced a more modern appearance (*top*) Lowland Scottish Leyland Tiger is shown here). In 1983, as described in 'Sellar's Market', the TC coach version was evolved. With changes mainly restricted to the front and rear, this effectively disguised the bus-like origins of the body (*above*) (this is an Alexander Midland Leyland Tiger, in Scottish Citylink livery). A further variation is the TS type, built for Central Scottish, a 53-seat service bus; it retains the external appearance, with top-sliders for ventilation (*overleaf*) (Kelvin Scottish's ex-Central Scottish Leyland Tiger). *SJB(2): Alexander (2)*

restyled the front end moulding, subtly altered the wheel arches, specified a plug door, and introduced gentle upsweep at the rear of the waistline. Of necessity, much of the work was cosmetic, but the finished effect was a successful transformation. Sellar admits that he would have liked to influence several other aspects, like livery, interior trim and detailing and window size.

Walter Alexander next came back to Dawson Sellar when a design for a double-deck coach was required. With the reawakened interest in these vehicles, several builders were looking at ways of offering suitable bodies. MCW chose to develop a complete vehicle, but other British builders preferred to adopt existing designs. Two Scottish Bus Group fleets, Eastern and Fife, were looking for double-deck coach bodies, on Leyland Olympian and Volvo Citybus respectively.

Here Sellar had greater freedom. The existing Alexander double-deck was the R type, an attractive design in the modern idiom. It already existed in lowheight and normal height forms, and this made the adaptation easier, for the Olympians were to be lowheight coaches and the Citybuses of necessity normal height.

Taking the R type as a base, Sellar developed a dramatic design that differed from other styles on the market, yet used a high proportion of existing parts. Most ingenious was perhaps the use of two R type windscreens, mounted above each other creating a distinctively-glazed front end appearance. There were touches of the TC body too, notably the front panel moulding and the wheel arch design. The overall effect was suitably impressive.

Since the RDC body Sellar has been involved in other projects for Alexander including a purposeful restyling of the front end of the ugly duckling P type bus body, and work on the front end and interior of the British Rail Class 143 built at Falkirk. Although the railcar work was restricted to these areas, Sellar has produced a front end thankfully free of the clutter that spoils so many of BR's recent multiple-units.

The end results suggest that calling in stylists can be a worthwhile investment for bodybuilders. For some of the more traditional firms, this may not be an easy step; engineers often have a deep-rooted suspicion of people with artistic flair — although the same may well be said the other way round.

In Build

Modern double-deck bus bodies are designed against the background of complex legislative requirements. The body must be strong and durable, but also of low weight to ensure that it can carry the maximum number of passengers within the 16-ton gross vehicle weight limit and within the axle weight limits too, often a critical area on rear-engined designs with their concentration of weight in the rear overhang. (This is why some double-deck buses have only four seats across the rear instead of the more usual five — the design is at the weight limit.) As a test of stability a double-deck bus has to be able to be tilted to an angle of 28° without falling over; therefore a low centre of gravity is necessary. There are tilt tables for this test at various locations in England and Scotland, which includes some major operators' premises. There are laid down minimum dimensions for many internal features — for example gangway widths, emergency exits, seat pitch — and on top of this there are the specific requirements of individual operators. These photographs, by courtesy of Leyland Bus, show the construction of bodies on Olympian chassis at Eastern Coach Works in Lowestoft.

Above:
This is the nearside of a long-wheelbase Leyland Olympian coach body. The body side frames are assembled in jigs and then given their internal panelling. The dark coloured sections have been treated with corrosion protection.

39

Above:
The roof is put together on a rotating jig to ease access. Alternate roof cross members will line up with the body side pillars when the roof and sides are united on the chassis.

Right:
This is the upper saloon floor being assembled. The dark-coloured brackets on every third cross member will be mated to the side pillars on the body. The cut-out area in the centre of the picture on the left is for the stair well.

Above:
The completed floor is covered in plywood before being fitted to the body shell.

Left:
The body sides, end and roof are brought together and mounted on the chassis at the end of a production line; glassfibre engine compartment covers are supplied with the chassis. Before starting to fit the body, the bodybuilder has to ensure that the chassis is standing completely level.

Below left:
The lower deck interior, looking forward, with the floor and staircase in position. This view illustrates how the upper deck floor is supported by the side pillars. This is a coach with forward-ascending staircase; another similar vehicle can be seen on the right.

Above:

As bodies proceed down the line they are fitted with electrical wiring, exterior panelling, interior trim panels on the sides and ceiling, and floor covering material, and they are given undercoat and topcoats of paint. ECW hand paints vehicles while builders of luxury coaches tend to use spray paints. Much of the front end panelling is of glassfibre; elsewhere aluminium panels are used.

Finally the completed shell is glazed, the interior trim is finished and the seating installed. This is a standard NBC Olympian with 77 moquette-trimmed seats; longitudinal seats are fitted over the wheel-arches. The rearward facing seat behind the staircase sits over part of the suspension.

Right:

The completed vehicle receives final attention in the finishing shop before being passed by ECW's own inspectors and by inspectors from the Department of Transport, who certify that the bus is roadworthy. Nearest the camera are a pair of Olympian buses with electronic destination displays, bound for Eastern National. The light-coloured lines on the windscreen are electric heating elements to aid demisting. The farthest vehicle is a semi-coach Olympian for Ribble.

Who's Who — UK

Although many well known names have disappeared from the British coachbuilding industry — and pessimistic observers expect more to go — British operators now have a wider choice of bodywork available to them than at any time in the past 30 years. Most of these are from luxury coachbuilders based in mainland Europe, some of which have been active in Britain for many years — Caetano, Jonckheere and Van Hool — while others are relative newcomers — such as Camo and Drogmöller.

The variety of bodywork available for service buses has diminished, but many of the coach body importers also build bus bodies and it would not be unreasonable to anticipate an upsurge of interest in imported bus bodies, particularly in the light of the Government's policy of privatisation of Britain's bus operators. Privately-owned companies feel less constrained than publicly-owned ones when it comes to following a policy of buying British products.

Virtually all of the coach bodies now being sold in Britain are based on welded structures built from square section tubular steel.

Most are assembled in jigs which are designed to ensure uniformity of quality in production, the use of steel combining high strength and comparatively low cost. Most coaches now feature bonded side windows (often double-glazed) and a single-stretched main body side panel. This applies equally to the builders of integral vehicles, which are also included in this section.

Bus bodies, by contrast, are normally made using aluminium alloy but with steel panelling — except where the bus bodybuilder is primarily a coachbuilder in which case welded steel tubes are more likely to be used. The main advantages of aluminium are reduced weight and greater corrosion resistance than steel. Its drawback is that it tends to be more expensive.

To avoid repetition, only the construction methods of those builders who deviate from these industry norms will be mentioned in the following résumé of the main coachbuilders currently active in Britain. Integral manufacturers are covered too, with, for the sake of completeness, brief details of the mechanical specifications of their products. Only builders of full-size vehicles are listed.

Alexander

The Alexander company has been building bus bodies in central Scotland since 1924. The present factory in Falkirk was opened in 1958.

Until the early 1960s the bulk of Alexander's output went to Scottish operators, but the introduction of stylish new single-deck (Y type) and double-deck (A type) bodies saw Alexander's products appear in increasing numbers in English (and some Welsh) fleets. These bodies enjoyed a long production life, albeit with many modifications, including the adoption of aluminium alloy construction from the early 1970s. The first major styling revisions to Alexander's bodywork did not occur until the early 1980s.

The first new body was the double-deck R type, introduced in 1980. This can be fitted to two- or three-axle chassis and can be supplied as a CKD kit for local assembly overseas. R types have been built on Leyland Atlantean (export only) and Olympian, Volvo Ailsa and Citybus, Dennis Dominator, Scania 112, Mercedes O.305 (export only) and MCW Metrobus in lengths of up to 12m and as low-height or full-height buses. An RDC double-deck coach body was introduced in 1984 using the basic R type frame but with a completely redesigned interior and exterior.

The dual-purpose T type body, which dated from 1974, was extensively restyled in 1983. The original model had a stepped roof over the first body side pillar and a blunt front end. Both these features disappeared on the revamped model which was available in three basic versions. There was a TS service bus, a TE express coach and a TC luxury coach. All

Above:
A normal-height Alexander R type body on a Dennis Dominator chassis in service with Kingston-upon-Hull City Transport. Curved glass windscreens are available as an option for both decks. *M. Fowler*

Above right:
The T type body by Alexander is a versatile product. This is a basic 11m-long TS type service bus delivered to Kelvin Scottish in 1985. It is based on a Leyland Tiger chassis. *SJB*

Right:
Alexander's P type has short bays and uses flat glass all round on this the original version. The window on the lower nearside corner panel is a practical feature which gives the driver a better view of the kerb. This is an East Midland Tiger, new in 1985. *A. R. Kaye*

had conventional rubber-mounted glazing, but bonded glazing was an option on the TC. The TC could also be supplied with a plug door in place of the standard jacknife type. Most pre-1983 T types were built on Leyland Leopards and Seddon Pennines while most of the restyled post-1983 examples have been on Leyland Tigers but with a few on Dennis Dorchesters for the Scottish Bus Group.

The last new design was the angular P type service bus body with flat glass all round and unusually short bays. The P type was designed with export orders in mind — although none has yet been received, and only a few P types have been sold in the UK. An improved front end was offered on the P type from 1986. P type bodies have been built on Dennis Lancet, Leyland Tiger and Volvo Citybus chassis.

Alexander remains the main body supplier to the Scottish Bus Group and has also supplied bodies to NBC and to various PTE and municipal fleets in the 1980s. Since 1975 the company has built up a significant business in the Far East, and with the sharp decline in home market bus orders in the 1980s it has also diversified into minibus conversions and the construction of railbus bodies, the first of which were delivered in 1985.

Alexander also has a factory in Belfast which builds single-deck bus bodies for Ulsterbus and Citybus and bodies for welfare buses, ambulances and fire engines.

Duple

Duple's history goes back to 1919 when the company commenced production of car bodies at Hornsey, north London. These bodies could be converted from cars to vans, hence the name Duple which comes from duplex — ie having two uses. The company moved to Hendon, northwest London, in 1926, where both double and single-deck bus bodies were built. In 1952 a base was established in Kegworth, Leicestershire, when Duple Motor Bodies (Midland) was set up to take over a small local coachbuilder, Nudd Brothers & Lockyer. Production was transferred to a new factory in nearby Loughborough in 1956. Willowbrook of Loughborough was taken over in 1958 and expansion continued with the takeover of H. V. Burlingham of Blackpool in 1960; the Blackpool company became Duple (Northern). The coachbuilding premises of W. S. Yeates in Loughborough were taken over in 1963 when Yeates ceased building bodies.

Ten years of expansion were then followed by some contraction. It was decided to concentrate production at Blackpool and the last bodies were built at Hendon in 1969/70. Next, Willowbrook was sold in 1971. In 1972 the first of the successful Dominant series bodies was introduced and by the mid-1970s production was approaching 1,000 bodies a year.

At the 1982 Motor Show Duple announced the replacements for the 10-year old Dominant coach design. (The Dominant bus continued unchanged.) There were two, the low-floor Laser and the high-floor Caribbean. Where most coachbuilders' high and low floor bodies shared a high degree of common parts and looked the same (apart from their

Below:
A late-model Duple Dominant — a Mk IV — for Southend Transport, on a Leyland Tiger chassis. *SJB*

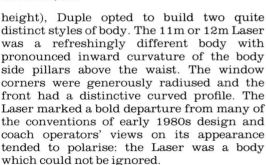

Above and right:
Caribbean comparison. The original Caribbean had four headlamps (although some later examples had only two) and a broad rubber strip round the skirt just above axle level. Rubber-mounted windows were used. Illustrated (*above*) is a Leyland Tiger for Derwent Coaches of Swalwell. The Caribbean II had a simpler front end and direct glazing, but only lasted a year. This (*right*) is a Southdown Leyland Tiger.
M. Fowler, SJB

height), Duple opted to build two quite distinct styles of body. The 11m or 12m Laser was a refreshingly different body with pronounced inward curvature of the body side pillars above the waist. The window corners were generously radiused and the front had a distinctive curved profile. The Laser marked a bold departure from many of the conventions of early 1980s design and coach operators' views on its appearance tended to polarise: the Laser was a body which could not be ignored.

The high-floor Caribbean — available only in 12m length — had a much squarer outline. The pillars were straighter, the front profile more upright and the windows — rubber mounted like those on the Laser — had squared-off corners. Neither body owed anything to previous Duple designs, except

around the rear end where the tail light assembly was carried over from the final Dominant models. The Caribbean body was, however, not quite what it seemed. Aware of the increasing pressure from imported integral coaches, Duple's engineers were working on their own integral and the fitment of the Caribbean body to conventional chassis was regarded as a stop-gap measure. In March 1983 Duple revealed its new Caribbean integral, saying that while the first 100 Caribbeans would be bodies on chassis, the integral was their real aim. The integral Caribbean was married up to a Neoplan N216 underframe fitted with a rear-mounted Mercedes engine. It had bonded glazing.

However, this project was doomed before production started. In May 1983 the Hestair group made a successful takeover bid for

Duple — which had lost almost £1 million on a £20 million turnover in the year to August 1982. Hestair already owned Dennis, whose output included bus and coach chassis, and could see advantages in having a strong link with a bodybuilder. The Caribbean integral was a victim of Hestair's reappraisal of Duple's future plans. The prototype remained unique.

The company was renamed Hestair Duple at the end of 1983. Early signs of the new ownership were the appearance of a few Caribbean-bodied Dennis Dorchesters in independent fleets and the re-equipping of the prototype integral with a Cummins L10 engine in place of the original Mercedes unit. A deal was concluded in 1983 with Moseley, the Midlands-based coach dealer, to build bodies on Bova underframes. This vehicle,

marketed as the Calypso, was effectively a low-height version of the Caribbean and was built only for the 1984 coach season, although a few remained unsold until 1985.

Despite new models and new management, Hestair Duple's sales were suffering from the influx of imported bodywork from continental Europe. Under Hestair management quality was improved and the workforce was reduced. At the 1984 Motor Show revised versions of the Laser and Caribbean were introduced. The basic body structures remained the same but both models were given an attractively restyled front panel with an integral aerofoil, direct glazing which eliminated the window-mounting rubbers, and simplified side trim. The Laser was given a one-piece windscreen and in both vehicles the interiors were extensively

redesigned. The restyling, by John Worker Design, gave rise to new model names — Laser 2 and Caribbean II.

Hestair had been busy on the integral front too, again in conjunction with John Worker Design. For coach operators the star of the 1984 Motor Show was the Integral 425, an all-new vehicle from Hestair Duple. The Integral 425 (the figure indicated its drag coefficient of 0.425) was a 12m long 3.36m high coach built on a welded steel spaceframe and powered by a rear-mounted 290bhp Cummins L10 engine which was linked to a ZF gearbox. It had air suspension which was *de rigeur* on any self-respecting 1980s coach, air brakes and the option of a Telma retarder. In the spring of 1985 the DAF 11.6-litre engine was offered as an alternative to the Cummins unit. Production started late in 1985.

Like the revamped Laser and Caribbean, the Integral 425 had direct glazing and a single-piece stretched side panel which was bonded to the frame. There was a large luggage locker in the wheelbase — Hestair Duple claimed 11cu m — with access by way of parallel-action vertically-lifting doors. The roof was a single-piece glassfibre panel and, in a clever marketing ploy, the vehicle was launched as a 63-seater. This, the highest capacity ever achieved in a British single-

deck coach, was obtained by fitting a new type of seat with a short squab. With conventional seating the Integral 425 did, of course, have the same capacity as any other well-designed 12m coach. An unusual front profile with a horizontally-split two piece windscreen set the Integral 425 apart from all other coaches on Britain's roads in 1985.

With the facelifted Caribbean and Laser and the new Integral 425, industry observers assumed that Hestair had completed its updating of the Duple range — and they were wrong. The 425 was in fact only the start of a new product range from Hestair Duple. In September 1985 a stylish new body — the 300 series — replaced both the Caribbean and the Laser after only three years in production and only one year in Laser 2 and Caribbean II form. Two versions of the new body were available, the low-floor 320 and the high-floor 340, with the figures indicating the vehicle height in centimetres. They overcame one of the problems of the previous range by sharing a high degree of parts commonality (around 60%). The 320 was offered in lengths of 11m and 12m for fitment to Bedford, DAF, Leyland and Volvo chassis. The 340 was only available on 12m-long DAF, Leyland and Volvo chassis. Four standards of trim were offered with the suffix letters L, SL, SLX or EX added to the basic body type designation as the standard of luxury improved. Thus the lowest-specification was the 320L, the highest the 340EX.

Duple has suffered more than rival Plaxtons from the 1980s invasion of continental coaches and in 1985 the company's production was around 300 units. However, under Hestair's management it now has one of the most distinctive ranges available with which to try to recover lost ground.

The Dominant

1972	Dominant launched
1974	Dominant bus introduced
1976	Dominant Goldliner prototype with slightly higher floor
1976	Dominant II — deep windscreen, shallow single-piece rear window
1976	Dominant E — bus seats in Dominant coach body shell
1980	Dominant III — as Dominant II but with shallow trapezoidal side windows
1980	Dominant IV — as Dominant II but with raised waistline and slightly shallower side windows
1981	Goldliner — high floor version of Dominant III and Dominant IV

East Lancashire Coach Builders

East Lancs was formed in Blackburn in 1938 and since 1963 has been part of the John Brown group. It is one of Britain's smallest builders of double-deck buses, its current output being under 100 a year.

With the flexibility inherent in small-scale production, East Lancs is able to build a number of variations on its basic double-deck theme. Particularly striking double-deck coach bodies have been delivered to a number of municipal fleets using the standard bus shell with revised front-end styling, bonded glazing, and new interior trim.

East Lancs was the first British builder to construct bodywork on the Dennis Dominator and on the Scania double-deck underframe. The company currently builds double-deck bodywork on these and on the Leyland Olympian and Volvo Citybus, as well as single-deckers on Leyland Tiger, Dennis Lancet and Dennis Falcon.

Most of East Lancs' customers are municipal fleets which have been particularly hard-hit by the 1980s cut-backs in public transport funding. Diversification at East Lancs has taken the form of bodies for tramcars for Blackpool Transport, the first of which was delivered in 1984, and minibus bodies, introduced in 1986.

Above right:

The lower overall height of the East Lancs coach body on the Leyland Olympian gives the vehicle a sleeker appearance. This is an Eastbourne example, delivered in 1985.

D. G. Savage

Right:

Typical of East Lancs' double-deck bodies is this example mounted on a Volvo Citybus for Plymouth. The downward slope of the front side window is an East Lancs feature, as is the curved one-piece front window on the upper deck which does not quite match the angular lines of the remainder of the body. Direct glazing is used.

G. R. Mills

Leyland Bus: Eastern Coach Works

Latterly part of Leyland Bus, ECW had the distinction of being Britain's biggest builder of double-deck bus bodies. Output in the late 1970s was over 600 a year — mostly for NBC. By 1986 production was almost half that number, with a different range of buyers including London Transport and a limited number of overseas customers. At the start of 1987 ECW, divorced from Leyland, was facing an uncertain future.

The present aluminium-framed double-deck body was introduced in 1980 and was a development of the integral Titan structure which Leyland's engineers had been working on in the mid-1970s. The ECW body was designed for Leyland's Olympian chassis and has evolved into high and low versions; short and long versions (the long one featuring a short bay in the centre); and bus and coach versions. The body is available with one or two doors and a choice of windscreens — double-curvature BET, flat glass, or curved Park Royal/London Country. Coach seats are available in the basic 9.5m-long bus shell but the first proper coaches, on long-wheelbase Olympian chassis, were for NBC and had fixed side windows and a rather untidy front-end design with the curved BET windscreen on the lower deck clashing with the flat raked screen on the upper deck. More recently a few double-deck coaches have been built, including some for export to Hong Kong and the USA, with greatly improved styling incorporating direct glazing and deep front windscreens of the type first used by Park Royal — in 1968 — for Manchester Corporation's Mancunians. Although it looks quite different from other ECW bodies the improved double-deck coach still uses the standard bus frame — albeit stretched to just over 11m.

Apart from the short-lived B51 coach body built for NBC in 1982, single-deckers have not featured prominently in ECW's output since the early 1970s, although a prototype for a new single-deck bus body was being developed in 1985.

ECW had a strong historic tie with NBC and one of its predecessors, the Tilling group, and it had really only been in the 1980s that it had made a strong effort to find new customers. ECW had some success in winning business in Scotland — particularly from Lothian Regional Transport, but also from the Strathclyde PTE and the Scottish Bus Group. The London Buses body order for 1986 was a major coup, although fewer other new English customers have been found — partly, of course, because fewer are buying new double-deckers in the mid-1980s.

Below left:

The standard ECW double-deck bus body as supplied to NBC on Leyland Olympian chassis is 13ft 8in (4.166m) high and has double-curvature BET windscreens. This is a United Automobile vehicle. *M. Fowler*

Below:

The Leyland Royal Tiger Doyen integral is available only as a high-floor model. The matt black area below the windscreen is intended to create the impression of a greater depth of glass. Crosville operates this coach. *M. Fowler*

Leyland Bus: Workington

Leyland's Workington plant was erected in 1970 to build the National, production of which ceased in the autumn of 1985. It now makes two integral vehicles — the Royal Tiger Doyen and the Lynx — while the ghost of the National lives on in the form of railbus bodies.

Production of the Royal Tiger Doyen got under way at the end of 1984 after a false start two years earlier at Leyland's Roe factory in Leeds. The Doyen is a 12m-long welded tubular steel integral coach. Two variants are offered, the Silver Crown and Gold Crown models with different standards of interior trim. The coach has a horizontal Leyland TL11 260bhp engine mounted at the rear and coupled to either a Leyland Hydracyclic or a ZF manual gearbox.

The first Lynx buses for the UK appeared at the beginning of 1986. The Lynx is 11.18m long and is a low-floor rear-engined service bus with an attractively-styled body which has direct glazing and flat glass wind screens. The driver's windscreen is angled back in a manner reminiscent of the Leyland bus body fitted to some Royal Tiger chassis in the early 1950s. Like the Royal Tiger Doyen, the Lynx is built of welded tubular steel, but on a channel-section underframe. It has a horizontal rear engine — Leyland or Gardner — and a Hydracyclic fully-automatic gear box. The Lynx is also aimed at export markets and an early prototype was sent to Australia for trials in 1985.

Railbuses are now an important part of Workington's business with an initial order for 100 Class 142s for 1985/86 being followed by a further 92 for 1986/87. A new production facility has been established for the manufacture of Class 15X heavy duty rail-cars.

Marshall

Marshall of Cambridge build small numbers of bus bodies for British operators. Traditionally these have been single-deckers but since 1978 Marshall has built double-deck bodies too, on Dennis Dominator, Leyland Atlantean and Olympian, Volvo Ailsa and Citybus, and Scania chassis for a range of customers. The distinctive single-deck Camair 80 body has been built on low-floor rear-engined and high-floor mid-engined chassis. Marshall also built the bodies on Bedford's stillborn JJL midibus of the late 1970s.

Marshall in the 1980s

Principal psv customers

Blackpool	Dennis Lancet
Bournemouth	Leyland Olympian
Darlington	Dennis Dominator (sd)
Derby	Volvo Ailsa, Volvo Citybus
Islwyn	Leyland Leopard
Leicester	Dennis Dominator (dd)
Newport	Scania 112 (dd)
South Yorkshire PTE	Leyland Atlantean
Tayside	Daimler Fleetline (sd, rebodied)
Thamesdown	Dennis Dominator (sd)

MCW

MCW developed during the 1970s from being a major builder of bodies on other makers' chassis to being an integral manufacturer. This was partly in response to a perceived threat from Leyland whose integral National effectively killed off demand for single-deck bus bodies in England and Wales and whose double-deck Titan, then under development as project B15, might have done the same for double-deck bodies. The Titan did not — it has come and gone — but MCW has found a small number of large fleet buyers for its Metrobus.

The aluminium-framed Metrobus, now only produced in its simplified Mk II version, is a two- or three-axle double-deck bus with rear-mounted Gardner, Rolls-Royce or Cummins engine and a Voith automatic gearbox. Its main buyers have been London Transport (which standardised on the original Mk I version), the West Midlands PTE and NBC. The original Metrobus was introduced in 1978 and is easily identifiable by its nearside windscreen which is a few inches deeper than that on the offside; the Mk II followed in 1982. The Mk II has a choice of curved or flat glass windscreens and can be fitted with one or two doors. A few have been equipped with high-backed coach seats in the

standard bus body shell. All British Metrobuses have been 9.5m long.

For the striking Metroliner double-deck coach launched in 1982 MCW found a ready market in NBC which now runs almost 100 of the type. This vehicle has three axles and a Cummins L10 engine. It is styled in the manner of continental European double-deck coaches with direct glazing and clean lines, but differs from them in being over 4m high. Various seating layouts are available with or without tables and a toilet compartment.

While the double-deck Metroliner has been a success, single-deck Metroliner coaches have fared less well. An angular standard-height body-on-chassis version launched in 1982 never got into volume production, while the integral Hi-Liner which followed it in 1983 has so far found only a few public sector customers and one in the private sector, despite efforts to interest independent operators in a British-built integral to rival Leyland's Royal Tiger Doyen and the various imported models. The Hi-Liner is a well-appointed luxury coach with all the features operators now expect in premium-quality coaches. It has a rear-mounted Cummins engine. All of the Metroliner models have tubular steel body frames.

Right and below:

These two Metrobuses show how a standard structure can be altered for different types of operation: the West Midlands PTE bus (*right*) has opening windows and flat glass windscreens; while the Reading Transport vehicle (*below right*) has fixed windows, high-backed seats and curved windscreens. Note also the different treatment of the ventilation louvres on the front to accommodate the offset number plate on the West Midlands bus.
J. G. Milnes, SJB

Below:

The double-deck Metroliner is available with a variety of trim options. This Wessex coach has a toilet, servery, reclining seats and a large rear luggage compartment. *A. R. Kaye*

Above:

The original single-deck Metroliner was an angular-looking coach with an asymmetric windscreen, at one time a MCW hallmark. Production only just got into double figures before a restyled model was introduced. This Strathclyde PTE vehicle has an unusual door arrangement to allow the carriage of passengers in wheelchairs. *SJB*

Above left and left:

The current Metroliner is available in standard or high-floor (Hi-Liner) versions. The Eastern National coach illustrates the standard model while the Northern Scottish vehicle is a Hi-Liner. Note the different location of the side moulding above the wheel-arches. Both vehicles have the same size of door which, if compared with the line formed by the top of windows, illustrates the height difference between the two models. Both use the same side windows, but have different windscreens.
G. R. Mills; D. G. Savage

Northern Counties

The Northern Counties Motor & Engineering Co (to give it its full title) is one of the oldest surviving builders of double-deck bus bodies. The company started operations in Wigan in 1919 and built its first double-deck bodies in 1928. Over the years Northern Counties has supplied bodies, mainly double-decked, to operators in most parts of Britain but with particularly strong support from municipal fleets in the northwest of England and from the independent Lancashire United Transport.

Changes in the structure of the bus industry coupled to a reduction in its size have seen Northern Counties become increasingly dependent on its major local operator, Greater Manchester Transport; the PTE now has a major shareholding in the company. A new body shop was built in Pemberton, Wigan, in 1980, alongside a site acquired in 1967 when Northern Counties took over the coachbuilding business of Massey Brothers. This new facility enabled all body construction to be done on one site — for many years part-completed bodies had to be driven across Wigan between Northern Counties' two separate works.

The bulk of Northern Counties' production — around 75% — is for Greater Manchester, principally on Leyland Olympian chassis. Other recent customers have included Chester (Dominators and Olympians), Southend (reconditioned Fleetlines), Cleveland (Dominators) and Nottingham, which takes bodies of a unique design, mostly on Volvo Citybuses. The first Northern Counties bodies to be supplied to London for some 40 years were delivered in 1984 on a batch of three trial Dennis Dominator chassis. Northern Counties has also secured some export business in the 1980s with the supply of built-up bodies on left-hand-drive Leyland Atlantean chassis to the Kuwait Transport Co.

After a gap of almost 10 years Northern Counties recommenced building single-deck bus bodies in 1985. These were on a batch of 22 rear-engined Dennis Domino midibus chassis for Greater Manchester Transport. Only 7.6m (25ft 2in) long and 2.28m (7ft 6in) wide, these were among the smallest bodies built by Northern Counties in postwar years. They were of particularly attractive appearance with bonded glazing, bonded side panels and a colour-keyed interior. The Midibus body was of welded steel construction, unlike the standard double-decker which used an aluminium alloy frame.

Northern Counties currently produces about 160 bodies a year and in 1986 diversified into minibus production.

Optare

Soon after Leyland Bus closed the Roe factory in Leeds in 1984 efforts were being made to revive it with the involvement of redundant employees and the West Yorkshire Enterprise Board. The old Roe factory started producing bus bodies again in 1985 with a slimmed-down workforce made up principally of former Roe employees who invested their redundancy payments in the new company, which is totally unconnected with Leyland.

The new company, Optare, offered a range of bodies for buses from midi-sized vehicles such as the Dennis Domino and Leyland Cub, through to double-deckers built to Roe designs by arrangement with Leyland. Recognising that the mid-1980s was not the

most auspicious time to start a business geared to building big buses, Optare also became involved in the building of ambulances and in the minibus market in which it offered both purpose-built bodies and less expensive van conversions. The first of these smaller PSV models appeared in 1986 and included the stylish CityPacer midibus body on MAN-VW chassis.

Plaxton

Plaxton of Scarborough commenced body-building — both cars and charabancs — soon after World War 1. Throughout the 1920s and 1930s the company built luxury coaches and in the mid-1930s a new factory was opened in Seamer Road to allow increased production. Coach bodybuilding ceased during World War 2 but recommenced at the end of 1945. The company branched out into single-deck bus bodywork with the introduction of the attractive Highway body in 1957. At this time Plaxton was one of four major coach bodybuilders supplying the British market — the others were Burlingham, Duple and Harrington. The turning point in Plaxton history — and the foundation of its present market leadership — was the introduction of the Panorama in 1958. This

featured long fixed windows for the first time in a British coach and marked a radical departure not only from previous designs from Plaxton but also from competing designs from other coachbuilders.

Plaxton increased its production capacity in 1961 by opening a new factory at Eastfield on the outskirts of Scarborough. Both the Eastfield and the Seamer Road works continue in use today. When Thurgood of Ware, a small coachbuilder in Hertfordshire, ceased body production in 1963 the premises were taken over by Plaxton for use as a southern service centre.

The Panorama was initially produced alongside conventional bodies with short windows and became increasingly popular during the 1960s. The body was revised in 1962 and again in 1964 but the first major

Right:
The original Paramount had a black plastic panel above the bright metal grille and headlamp surround, and a break in the waist moulding below the feature window — clearly visible on the right-hand coach in this shot of a pair of Tigers for Finglands of Manchester. They have 3500 bodies. *Leyland*

Below right and bottom:
The Mk II Paramounts have a cleaner front end and a continuous waist moulding. They also have small Plaxton badges below the windscreen. The Grey Green Volvo B10M has a 3500 body with a horizontally split windscreen and large radial-arm wipers, while the Green Line Tiger has a 3200 body with a vertically split windscreen and, in consequence, pantograph wipers. *SJB, D. G. Savage*

change came in 1968 with the Panorama Elite which had deeper windows with curved glass — another British first for Plaxton. Bus body production continued throughout this period, albeit on a fairly small scale.

The Elite was replaced by the steel-framed Supreme in 1974 and this was joined in 1976 by the Viewmaster, the first British-built high-floor coach body. The Viewmaster's extra height gave passengers a better view and provided additional luggage space. This helped to overcome a growing problem with 12m-long coaches which were able to carry more passengers than 11m-long vehicles but offered little or no extra luggage capacity. The Supreme had even deeper curved windows than the Elite — except for the short-lived and rather unattractive Supreme

VI which had shallow flat glass side windows and was Plaxton's somewhat inadequate answer to Duple's Dominant III.

Bus body production had effectively ceased in the late 1970s but was revived with the announcement of the Bustler in 1980. As in the past, bus bodies in the 1980s continued to account for a very small part of Plaxton's output.

Plaxton's current model, the Paramount, was launched at the 1982 Motor Show and represents evolutionary design with its obvious Plaxton 'look'. The Paramount was in fact quite different from the Supreme and Viewmaster which it replaced, with a squarer outline around the cantrail and with shallower square-cornered windows. A stretched steel side panel was fitted. The Paramount was launched in two basic versions, the 3200 and 3500, with the figures indicating the overall height in millimetres. The lower body was available in lengths from 8m to 12m; the higher body was initially offered only on 12m chassis. A star rating system was introduced to differentiate between groups of options offering increased luxury.

While Duple was losing £1 million in 1982, Plaxton was making £1.1 million on a £24.8 million turnover and this profit was almost trebled in the following year to £2.92 million. However, Plaxton, like Duple, was hit by the twin blows of low-priced continental imports and the general business recession. Production in 1985 was down to around 650 units compared with almost double that number in 1979.

At the 1982 Motor Show Plaxton had displayed a stylist's model of a double-deck coach and this was launched in January 1984 as the Paramount 4000. Again the figure indicated the overall height in millimetres. The 4000 was based on a Neoplan N722 underframe powered by a 352bhp Mercedes V10 engine coupled to a ZF HP600 six-speed fully-automatic gearbox. It had three axles, independent front suspension and could carry up to 83 passengers. It was, of course, Plaxton's first ever double-decker. The 4000 bore a strong family resemblance to the other Paramounts and had bonded glazing — a feature which appeared at the beginning of 1985 on the Mk II Paramount 3200 and 3500.

For 1985 Gardner's new 320bhp 15.5-litre 6LYT engine was offered as an option in the 4000 along with an eight-speed manual ZF gearbox.

The Mk II Paramounts had restyled front panels, bonded glazing as an option, new wheel trims, and a completely new interior with deep luggage racks incorporating trunking for optional air conditioning. The racks could be supplied with aircraft-type doors. New deeper windscreens were offered on chassis with a low driving position — these models were the 3200ls Mk II and the 3500ls MkII, with 'ls' indicating low screen. (Deep windscreens on the 3200 body had in fact first appeared in 1984 on a batch of Quest 80 chassis for Excelsior of Bournemouth.) The next all-new model was the Paramount 4000RS (Rear Saloon) which was the first British-built twin-deck body and was designed for fitment to mid-engined three-axle chassis. The first 4000RS bodies were built at the beginning of 1985 on Volvo B10MT chassis, and seated 64 passengers with space for over 13cu m of luggage. A further double-deck development was the fitment of the 4000 body to the rear-engined Scania K112TR chassis in the autumn of 1985. This variant was known as the 4000MS.

Plaxton's 1986 range was the most comprehensive available from a British builder and comprised the following Paramount models:

Type	Length	To fit
3200 Mk II	8m-12m	Bedford Y, Leyland Tiger, Scania K112CR, DAF SB, DAF MB, Volvo B10M, ACE Puma
3200ls Mk II	10m-12m	Volvo B10M, Leyland Tiger, DAF SB, Scania K112CR, ACE Puma
3500 Mk II	11m-12m	Leyland Tiger and Royal Tiger, DAF MB, DAF SB, Mercedes O.303, Scania K112CR, Volvo B10M
3500ls Mk II	11m-12m	Leyland Tiger, Volvo B10M, Scania K112CR, DAF SB
4000RS	12m	Volvo B10MT
4000MS	12m	Scania K112TR
4000	12m	Neoplan N722

In addition the Supreme remained available for fitment to the front-engined Bedford PJK(VAS) and the Bustler body was still in production. A Mini-Supreme body for fitment to small Mercedes chassis was in small-scale production by Plaxton's service division.

Reeve Burgess

Reeve Burgess and its predecessors have a long history of bodybuilding, but have only comparatively recently achieved prominence in the bus industry, largely as a result of the stylish coach-built Reebur minicoach bodies made in the late 1970s and early 1980s. Reeve Burgess still produces coach-built bodies, mainly on midi-sized chassis such as the MAN MT and Leyland Cub, although big bodies have been built on short-wheelbase Leyland Tigers and on a 12m-long Dennis Dorchester. With small-scale production Reeve Burgess offers bespoke bodies for smallish vehicles which can range from welfare buses through to luxury coaches; when building the latter the company can benefit from the experience of Plaxton, its parent company since 1980.

Reeve Burgess also produces coach conversions of panel vans (notably the larger Mercedes models) and crew cabs for trucks.

Above:
Typical of Reeve Burgess' coachbuilt bodywork is this Riviera, based on a front-engined MAN chassis. *SJB*

Wadham Stringer

Wadham Stringer (Coachbuilders) operates from a four-acre site in Waterlooville, near Portsmouth. Wadhams, one of the predecessors of the present company, had a long history of bus and coach bodybuilding but Wadham Stringer's current involvement dates back to the late 1970s when it took over the coachbuilding activities of Sparshatts, which had been active in the supply of small welfare buses and ambulances to local authorities, hospitals and other similar organisations.

Wadham Stringer — still building ambulances and welfare buses — decided to tackle the real bus market and to do so abandoned the utilitarian designs inherited from Sparshatts, replacing them with the completely new Vanguard which was announced at the end of 1979. The first Vanguard body, built from the outset to meet the British PSV Construction & Use regulations, was mounted on the new Leyland Cub chassis and was used as a demonstrator at the 1979 Scottish Motor Show. The Cub was not such a strange choice of chassis as it might appear. Wadham Stringer was keeping its traditional welfare market very much in mind, a market in which both the Cub and the Wadham Stringer Vanguard have been extremely successful.

The Vanguard is a neat body with a welded steel frame, a distinctive deep windscreen, deep flat glass side windows, and a shallow roof line with a pod at the rear. Customers are offered a wide choice of interior layouts ranging from coach seats (with fixed windows and forced air ventilation) to removable bus seats with wheelchair anchorage points and a tail lift, in which form the body is marketed as the Vantage. A face-lifted coach — model Vanguard II — was added to the range in 1986.

Above:
Wadham Stringer has supplied Vanguard bodies on a wide range of chassis. Among independent operators, A1 Service of Ardrossan has two with coach-type seats on Leyland Tiger chassis. *SJB*

A feature of the Vanguard is its flexibility. It is available in lengths from 7m to 12m and a narrow 2.3m (7ft 6in wide) version is offered as well as the standard 2.5m (8ft 2½in) wide model. Vanguards have been built on front-engined chassis (Leyland Cub, Ford R, Volvo B57, Dodge Commando, MAN, Bedford PJK and NJM), underfloor-engined chassis (Dennis Lancet, Leyland Leopard and Tiger, Bedford Y, Bristol LHS, Volvo B58) and rear-engined chassis (Dennis Falcon, Scania 112, Ward Dalesman). Much of Wadham Stringer's output is for non-PSV operators.

Willowbrook

Willowbrook of Loughborough was a major bodybuilder in Britain until the early 1970s when its fortunes slowly began to decline. At this period, newly independent from Duple which had owned the company since 1958, Willowbrook was still building double-deck bodies, although in declining quantities, and single-deck bus bodies, usually on light-duty chassis for independents. The company was also an active exporter.

The new Spacecar coach body, launched in 1975, was quite different from the chrome-and-glitter products of most other manufacturers at that time but failed to catch the imagination of coach operators. It was developed into the much more mundane 001 design and Willowbrook's last big order was for a batch of 003 bodies on Leyland Leopard chassis for NBC in 1980. By 1984 Willowbrook had virtually closed down but it was re-formed and in 1985, operating from new premises in Loughborough, introduced a totally new coach body — the Crusader. This was built to the sort of specification which coach operators expected in the mid-1980s welded steel structure, direct glazing, one piece main body side panel, soft interior trim. A prototype built on a Bedford chassis was shown to operators in the autumn of 1985.

Right:
The prototype Willowbrook Crusader has clean lines. It was a demonstrator on a Bedford chassis. *SJB*

Above:
The Wright TT bus body has a distinctively angular front end and has been bought by Maidstone, Ulsterbus and, as shown here, Arran Coaches. Flat glass is used to minimise replacement costs in the event of damage. *SJB*

Wright

Wright of Ballymena is the smaller of Northern Ireland's two coachbuilders and, until 1980, specialised in the production of conventional small bodies for school buses, as well as building van bodywork. In 1980 Wright concluded a licensing agreement with Swiss Aluminium, generally known as Alusuisse, to build bodywork using Alusuisse designs. Most conventional bodies make extensive use of steel or aluminium tubes or sections but the Alusuisse system uses a range of standard interlocking extrusions, one of which forms the main body side panel below the waist. The panel above the windows is also an aluminium extrusion. The advantages claimed for the Alusuisse system are ease of assembly, low weight, high strength and longer life. The disadvantages cited by conventional builders are reduced design flexibility and the high cost of the aluminium extrusions.

Wright's first Alusuisse bodies — known as the TT — were for a traditional customer, the local education authority, and were fitted to Bedford VAS and YMT chassis. They were of attractive but essentially utilitarian appearance and had a distinctive three-piece flat glass windscreen. A demonstrator was built and subsequently sold to Maidstone Borough Transport which later ordered TT bodies from Wright. The only other TT sales to PSV operators have been to Arran Coaches, in Scotland, and to Ulsterbus. One of the two Ulsterbus vehicles was fitted with coach seats and in this configuration was called the Royal.

Meanwhile Wright had been developing a coach version of its body, working in close co-operation with Bedford's styling department. This retained the basic TT structure but with a dramatically restyled front end and a new roof profile. It was launched as the Contour at the end of 1982 and was one of the most distinctive coach bodies available in Britain at that time. Clever use of tinted glazing concealed the radiused corners of the

63

main side window pans and the use of black plastic materials around the front end gave the appearance of a very deep windscreen. The rear wheels were partially enclosed (this became an option on later bodies) and attractive wheel trims were fitted. The exterior shape with its steeply raked windscreen was developed using wind tunnel tests to minimise drag.

Internally Wright offered all the options expected by coach operators including carpets and a choice of seating layouts. The type numbers 385 and 485 indicate different levels of trim. The driver's area was particularly attractive, benefiting again from Bedford's styling experience. At the rear, a cantilevered boot door which lifted parallel to the body — instead of being top-hinged — was an unusual and practical option. Wright also offered side access doors to the boot.

Initial production was on Bedford YNT chassis and an early customer was Whittle of Highley, a confirmed Bedford user. The Contour has since been made available on other chassis and examples can be seen on Leyland Tiger, ACE Puma and Ford R series in lengths ranging from 8m to 12m. A high-floor version of the Contour is under development.

The Contour is a low-volume product from a small manufacturer — annual output can be measured in tens rather than in hundreds — but it has demonstrated how a small coachbuilder can find a place in the highly competitive British coach market.

Below:
The Contour is built using the same methods as the TT but with quite different styling. Flush-mounted glazing disguises the curved corners of the window sections, just visible on the top corners of the offside windows in this photograph. This is a Bedford of Alpine Travel of Llandudno — most Contour bodies have been built on Bedfords. *K. Lane*

Who's Who — Imports

Berkhof

Berkhof has been supplying coach bodies to British operators through Ensign Bus, the well known Essex dealer, since 1983. Berkhof bodies are now built in a modern factory in Valkenswaard, Holland, which was opened in the spring of 1985. Berkhof has in fact only been building coach bodies since 1971 and its new factory gives it the capacity to build up to 140 coaches a year with well over half of the company's output being destined for British operators.

Berkhof's bodies follow curent European practice, being of jig-built welded construc-tion with a stretched single-piece main body side panel and a wide range of options on a basic theme. The standard models are the Esprite (3.4m and 3.5m high) and Everest (3.7m high) and these feature tinted win-dows, electrically-controlled adjustable heated rear-view mirrors, reclining seats and a Webasto auxiliary heater. The Everest has a horizontally-split two-piece windscreen. An option pioneered by Ensign is the removable sunken toilet: the toilet compartment is designed in two parts and the upper part from the level of the saloon floor can be

Above left:
A strong family resemblance runs through the Berkhof range which starts with this midicoach based on the Iveco 315 rear-engined chassis and marketed in Britain as the Elk. This is a 28-seat demonstrator. *G. R. Mills*

Left:
The standard 12m-long Esprite, on a Volvo B10M for Wallace Arnold. *G. R. Mills*

removed and replaced by a flat floor panel. This allows extra seats to be fitted when the toilet is not required — without disturbing the plumbing installation for the WC and wash basin which remain *in situ* hidden under the floor. This feature has since been copied by most other builders. The Esprite and Everest bodies are available on Leyland Tiger, Volvo B10M, DAF MB and SB and rear-engined Scania, MAN and Mercedes-Benz chassis.

Moving up the range there is the Emperor III, a twin-deck 64-seater available on Volvo's three-axle B10MT chassis (although the original Emperors were built on standard two-axle B10Ms). This is 3.95m high and has a rear lower saloon (with closed-circuit television camera to keep the area under the driver's view) and seats at the front above the driving compartment. Ensign's flagship — no pun intended — is the 76-seat Eclipse double-decker on Scania K112TR chassis. At

Above:

This top-of-the-range Eclipse on a Scania K112TR for Charter Coach of Great Oakley is a 76-seater — three times the capacity of the Elk. Windscreen wipers are provided for the upper deck. *G. R. Mills*

the other end of the Berkhof range Ensign offers the Elk, a midicoach based on the rear-engined Iveco 315 chassis.

Where most importers of coach bodies are selling almost exclusively to independents, Ensign has succeeded in selling Berkhof bodies to major public sector operators including London Country Bus Services, Western Scottish and Southend Transport. In 1984 Ensign supplied London Transport with its first modern coach, a DAF on lease for trial operation.

Bova

Bova is one of the smallest manufacturers whose integral coaches are being imported to Britain. The company has an annual output of around 250 units from its plant at Valkenswaard, Holland.

The standard Bova is the integral Futura with its unusually-shaped bulbous front, said to improve aerodynamic efficiency. It is a 12m-long rear-engined coach and is available in two heights — the 3.275m FLD which gives up to 9cu m of luggage space and the 3.515m FHD which gives up to 12cu m of luggage space. While the construction and trim of both models is similar, the FLD uses DAF's 8.25-litre engine, while the FHD uses the same maker's 11.6-litre unit, available as an option in the FLD. Mercedes-powered models are also available and are coded FLM and FHM.

The Futura, introduced to Britain in 1983, replaced the previous Europa models which had deeper side windows and a more upright front. They used the smaller DAF engine and were available in Britain from 1981 to 1985.

Bova also produces for sale in Holland a low-floor integral citybus, the X-press, which uses a horizontal DAF 11.6-litre engine and can carry up to 90 passengers.

Below and bottom:
Two styles of Bova Futura in NBC service. The Shamrock & Rambler vehicle in the livery of the Bournemouth Orchestras is a low-floor FLD; the Crosville coach is a high-floor FHD. The flat-glass side windows are the same on both models but the FHD has a much deeper windscreen. *M. Fowler; K. Lane*

Caetano

Portuguese builder Caetano has been selling coach bodies in the UK since 1967. The early vehicles were, to say the least, flamboyant and although they sold well cannot be said to have achieved universal acceptance with their unusual lines and paint schemes.

The current Algarve, introduced in 1983, has given Caetano a new image. Gone is the Iberian styling and in its place is an attractively curved European coach body available with all the features British operators have come to expect of imported coach bodywork. Caetano coach bodies are currently available on Bedford, DAF, Leyland and Volvo chassis, depending on the body model.

A new Caetano bus body, the Stagecoach, was introduced in 1985 with an eye on the impending deregulation of local bus services in 1986 and an anticipated upsurge of interest in service buses from small operators. The Stagecoach is a 57-seat 12m-long body of attractively angular appearance and is mounted on a Volvo B10M chassis on which the frame layout allowed a reasonably low floor and a wide front entrance.

Two other new Caetano products announced in 1985 were coach-built midi vehicles: the Optimo, based on a Toyota Coaster chassis, and the Iveco-based Viana. Both models are front-engined and have deep windows and a low waistline, which sets them apart from most other vehicles in their class. The Iveco has a set-back front axle which allows a proper front entrance, thus making the vehicle suitable for use on bus services.

The Algarve range

N-NDH 3.065m high, 12m long
N-SDH as N-NDH but with low driving position
R-NDH 3.165m high, 9.7m or 12m long
R-SDH as R-NDH but with low driving position
H-NDH 3.265m high, 12m long
H-SDH as H-NDH but with low driving position
X-NDH 3.465m high, 12m long
X-SDH as X-NDH but with low driving position

Above:
Caetano's Optimo is a stylish midibus or coach based on the Toyota Coaster chassis; the Iveco-based Viana is of broadly similar appearance. Note the windows which are unusually deep for a body of this size. *SJB*

Above:
The Stagecoach service bus body, a totally new design, was launched in Britain in 1985. The **prototype had fixed windows and was on a 12m-long Volvo B10M chassis.** *Caetano*

Camo

In 1985 Ensign Bus announced that Portuguese Camo bodywork would be available from the company in Britain from 1986. Camo's high-floor body is of particularly distinctive appearance with sculpted side panels which make a welcome change from the generally flat-sided bodies offered by most builders. Camo bodywork has not previously been available in Britain.

Drogmöller

A Drogmöller integral coach was exhibited at the 1984 Motor Show and was noteworthy for its unusual sloping waistline which made the side windows considerably deeper at the front of the coach than at the rear. In 1985 Drogmöller announced that it would be making a more conventional straight-waisted integral, the E320, available in Britain — at a price of over £100,000 . . . Drogmöller uses Mercedes-Benz units.

Top:
A Camo-bodied Scania in the fleet of Portuguese operator Rodoviaria Nacional. Similar bodies are to be imported to the UK by Ensign Bus. *SJB*

Left:
The first British Drogmöller had this eye-catching sloping waistline and was delivered to Bergland of Watford in 1985.
T. W. Moore

Ikarus

Hungarian bus and coachbuilder Ikarus, the biggest manufacturer in Europe, will be selling coach bodies in Britain from 1987 through the Kirkby dealership. Ikarus al[...] announced plans to establish a manufactu[...]ing base in the UK.

Irizar

Spanish-built Irizar bodywork has been offered intermittently on the British market since the late 1970s. The current Pyrenean body was announced in 1983 but, although it was a marked improvement on its predecessors, annual sales have yet to reach double figures. A less expensive body with simpler trim, the Shetland, was introduced to tl[...] British market in 1984.

Below:
Irizar's restrained Pyrenean has sold in small[...] numbers. This one is on a Volvo B10M for Provence Private Hire of St Albans.
S. C. Morris

Jonckheere

Jonckheere is one of Europe's oldest coachbuilders, having commenced in 1881 as a builder of horse-drawn carriages. The company is Belgian and its factory is in the town of Roeselare, from which the firm's former UK sales company took its name. Jonckheere sold small numbers of coach bodies in Britain in the early 1970s but it was only with the establishment of Roeselare Sales as an exclusive British distributor in 1980 that Jonckheere became a significant force in Britain, quickly overtaking Van Hool and Caetano to become the biggest supplier of imported bodywork in this country.

The current Jubilee range was launched in 1981, the company's centenary year, and has evolved into a trend-setting range of bodies introducing novel seating layouts to British travellers. Most of Jonckheere's designs have been imitated by its competitors — and imitation remains the sincerest form of flattery. In Britain Jonckheere pioneered the twin-deck concept for mid-engined coache[...] in which a small lower deck seating area [...] provided behind the rear axle. This, the P9[...] has since been copied by other builder[...] Jonckheere was also the first builder t[...] provide a double-deck coach body with mid-saloon separate from the driving are[...] with its P99 body on the DAF SBR three-ax[...] rear-engined chassis. A less successf[...] innovation was the small Piccolo P35, base[...] on a modified rear-engined Quest 80 chassi[...] This was announced in 1984 but few wer[...] built and even fewer were sold when Quest 8[...] went into liquidation in 1985. Roeselar[...] Sales, too, ceased trading in 1985 an[...] Jonckheere formed a new British subsidiar[...] to sell its bodywork.

Jonckheere bodies are available on mo[...] chassis builders' products and although onl[...] coach bodies were sold in Britain until 198[...] the company also builds bus bodies for othe[...] markets, and made its first British bus sale[...] in 1986.

The current British range consists of:

P35   midi-coach body
P50   3.5m high single-deck 12m coach
P599 3.5m high single-deck 12m coach
      with low driving position
P90   high-floor 12m coach with rear
      lower saloon
P95   high-floor 12m three-axle coach with
      rear lower saloon
P99   double-deck 12m three-axle coach

Below:
**The 12m-long P599 has a low driving position,
as shown on this Volvo B10M operated by
National Travel (East).** *G. R. Mills*

Bottom:
**The P99 double-decker has a centre door and is
based on the three-axle DAF SBR2300 rear-
engined underframe. This one was bought by
Young's of Cambridge.** *G. R. Mills*

LAG

Coach bodies from LAG first appeared in Britain at the end of 1982 and they were followed 12 months later by a DAF-powered integral. LAG bodies are imported from Belgium and to consolidate the company's position in the UK, LAG bought a British dealer in 1985 to handle future sales.

LAG builds about 100 bodies a year and also makes commercial vehicle trailers and tanker bodies, and a three-axle midibus or midicoach, the Tristar. This was first shown in the UK in 1982 and has a Mercedes engine and air suspension. Few have been sold.

The LAG coach body — so far offered only in 12m-long form — is known as the Galaxy and has been fitted to DAF, Leyland and Volvo chassis for the British market. The integral, also only available in 12m form, is sold as the LAG Panoramic and can be distinguished from the otherwise similar Galaxy by its more upright front end profile. For 1986 LAG was advertising integral based on the Galaxy, and Panoramic bodywork for conventional chassis, thus making model identification more difficult.

Above:
LAG's Galaxy body on a Leyland Tiger in the fleet of Osborne of Tollesbury. LAG's deep windscreen gives the body a more distinctive appearance than many of its European competitors. *G. R. Mills*

Below:
The LAG Panoramic integral has a much more upright front than the Galaxy. This example was for Marchwood Motorways of Southampton. *S. C. Morris*

MAN

MAN is a German company whose mid-1970s brochure said quaintly: 'Bus operators and public bus services give high notes to MAN buses because these vehicles are of technically-matured and future-oriented design.' These remarks presumably apply equally to MAN coaches and it was with the future-oriented SR series that MAN became the first of the current group of continental integral manufacturers to enter the UK. That was in 1979, since when MAN has sold over 100 SR240 and SR280 coaches. The difference between these models is the engine, naturally-aspirated at 240bhp in the former and turbocharged at 280bhp in the latter. Both engines are by MAN and most British MANs have been SR280s.

The MAN SR is a rear-engined coach of distinctive appearance. The bonded side windows are unusual among imported coaches in that they are of flat glass. The body sides are almost vertical and the roof is flat with little curvature at its edges, all of which gives the MAN a solid squared-off look. Although shorter versions have been sold in Germany, only the 12m-long model has been imported to Britain.

From the start MAN aimed at the top end of the luxury coach market with a choice of reclining or fixed seats and the availability of a toilet and servery. Standard features included double-glazing, side window blinds, a driver's door with built-in wardrobe, a Webasto oil-fired heater, an offside continental exit door, an adjustable steering column, a heated driver's side window, headlamp wash/wipe, and 9.3cu m of luggage space in the wheelbase. A Highliner, 8in (20.3cm) taller than the original model, was added to the range in 1983.

An updated model, the SR362, with less angular front and rear ends and an improved interior specification, was released in Germany in 1985 and in Britain at the end of 1986; SR280 sales in Britain ceased during 1985.

MAN also produces a range of rear-engined city buses — single-deck, double-deck and articulated — of which only the articulated model has been seen in Britain.

Below:
The MAN SR280, seen here in the livery of Beavis of Bussage, has been superseded by the structurally similar SR362 which has smoother frontal styling. The first British SR362s arrived for the 1986-87 coach season.
G. R. Mills

Mercedes-Benz

Mercedes-Benz sells only one full-size fully-imported coach in Britain, the 12m-long O.303 integral. Although various Mercedes coaches have been sold intermittently since the late 1960s, it was only with the appointment of a UK distributor — W. S. Yeates — in 1983 that Mercedes started active marketing in Britain. The O.303 is quite an old design — it was launched in Germany in 1974 — but it is available to a very high specification and, of course, has the cachet of the three-pointed star emblem on the front.

The O.303 is not perhaps the most attractive of coaches, having a high waist-line, heavy-looking window mountings (no direct glazing here) and windows which curve into the roof line. The original right-hand drive high-floor model was joined in Britain by a standard-height vehicle at the end of 1985.

The O.303 has a rear-mounted Mercedes engine.

Neoplan

Neoplan's distinctive rear-engined integral coaches were launched in Britain at the 1980 Motor Show. Four models from Neoplan's extensive range are currently available in Britain. The most popular is the three-axle double-deck Skyliner N122 with its distinctive raked upper deck windscreen and its sloping body pillars — sometimes unkindly referred to as juke box styling. The N122 is comprehensively equipped and can carry up to 77 seated passengers while still providing space for a toilet, a driver's bunk, a small servery and 10cu m of luggage. The standard Skyliner drive-line is a 355bhp Mercedes OM423 V10 engine linked to a ZF manual gearbox; at the 1984 Motor Show Neoplan announced the option of a British engine — the Gardner 6LYT 330bhp unit. A two-axle version of the Skyliner, the N122/2 Clubliner, is also available. This seats 49 in the upper deck and eight in the lower deck, which also incorporates a lounge area.

The other models are two-axle single-deck coaches bearing a strong family resemblance to the double-deckers. These have sloping pillars and side windows with a pronounced curve at roof level. The N116 Cityliner is a high-floor (3.55m) model with 49 seats, toilet and 11cu m of luggage space in the wheelbase. It has a horizontally-split two-piece windscreen with an upright lower section and a raked upper section. The two screens are divided at the level of the lower dge of the main body side windows and the ivision carries the waistline round the front f the vehicle. The N117 Spaceliner is ffectively a through-deck Cityliner with eats above a lowered driving position. The lightly lower (3.35m) N216H Jetliner has a aked single-piece windscreen and is the earest any Neoplan design comes to looking estrained.

Revised frontal panels were being gradually introduced to the Neoplan range in 985 and first appeared on British models in 986.

Neoplan also builds citybuses, although one are available in Britain. For many years he standard power for Neoplan buses and oaches was Mercedes; however, at the end of 982 Mercedes indicated that it was no onger prepared to supply engines for ompetitors' citybuses and Neoplan buses are now offered with the choice of Deutz or DAF engines, while the DAF 11.6-litre DKT and the Scania 11-litre DS11 are now offered in British Jetliners, with Mercedes engines available as an alternative — although they remain standard in the other Neoplan models.

The full-size Neoplans are built in Stuttgart and are complemented by the 27-seat N907 Uniliner, built in West Berlin. The Uniliner is 7.25m long and is front-engined (MAN or Mercedes). Only a small number have been sold in Britain.

Neoplan's range is much wider than its British sales would suggest and includes single and double-deck citybuses, articulated buses and coaches, and even an 18m-long articulated double-deck coach. As well as having factories in Germany, Neoplan builds buses in the USA and in Ghana.

Above left and Above:
Two coaches from the Perth-based Stagecoach fleet — one of Neoplan's best British customers — illustrate Neoplan styling. The single-decker is a Jetliner which looks very similar to the top deck of the double-deck Skyliner. The Skyliner design has changed little since 1973 and was face-lifted, along with other models in the range, for 1986. The newer models have a neater front panel below the windscreen. *SJB*

Above:
Short wheelbase Jetliners are available but are rare in Britain. This one was delivered to Beavis of Bussage in 1984. *G. R. Mills*

Ramseier & Jenzer

Who, you may well ask, are Ramseier & Jenzer? They are a Swiss builder whose bodywork is fitted to the Volvo C10M integral. The low-volume high-specification C10M was first shown in Britain at the 1984 Motor Show and is marketed as a complete vehicle by Volvo, which is why the Ramseier & Jenzer name is little known in Britain. Most of the company's output — around 80 bodies a year — is sold on the Swiss market.

Above:
Ramseier & Jenzer bodywork is fitted to Volvo's stylish C10M. This is a left-hand-drive prototype. *Volvo*

The C10M is comprehensively equipped and has a mid-mounted Volvo engine and a stainless-steel underframe to which the Ramseier & Jenzer body is fitted.

Setra

Kässbohrer, maker of Setra integral coaches and a wide range of commercial vehicle bodies, has a history going back to 1893. The current 200 series Setra coach models were launched in Germany in 1976 and in Britain at the end of 1981. Setra coaches have a reputation for quality which is underlined by five successive Coach of the Year awards at the Brighton Coach rally from 1982 to 1986.

The standard British market Setras are built at Ulm and are the S215H and the S215HD, which are 12m long and 3.09m and 3.34m high respectively. Apart from the difference in height, both bodies are gen-erally similar. The S215HD has a centre sunken toilet, centre continental door and 49 reclining seats whereas the lower S215H has 53 reclining seats, a rear continental door and no toilet. Setras are expensive, and in an attempt to broaden their appeal a less expensive model ('cheaper' somehow seems inappropriate), built in Kässbohrer's French plant, was sold in Britain in 1983/84. The French plant, at Ligny-en-Barrois, was commissioned in 1981 and builds the S215HR Rational which sold in Britain at a price not quite 10% below the standard S215H. It shared the running units of its more expensive brothers — Mercedes OM422

Right:
The Setra Imperial is one of the most expensive coaches available in Britain. This one, operated by Townsend Thoresen, won the 1985 Brighton Coach Rally.
G. R. Mills

naturally-aspirated 280bhp V8 engine, ZF S6-90 six-speed manual gearbox and independent front suspension — but with conventional drum brakes in place of the unconventional (for a coach) disc brakes used on the front wheels of the Ulm-built bodied coaches. However, the body of the S215HR was completely different with, instead of direct glazing, rubber-mounted flat-glass windows with a hopper-type opening top section, something not seen on a British coach body for many years. The frontal profile was also more upright than on the Ulm-built coaches, giving the vehicle something of a 'service-coach' appearance.

The most expensive Setra to appear in Britain has been the 4m-high three-axle double-deck S228DT Imperial, launched in Germany in 1981 and in Britain in 1982 and priced at over £150,000. This uses a more powerful Mercedes V8 engine, the turbocharged and intercooled OM422LA which produces 375bhp, and a heavier-duty ZF manual gearbox, the eight-speed ZF4S-150GP. But otherwise it has much in common with other 200-series coaches in terms of its design, construction and appearance. Setra's British range is completed by the S210H, a 9m coach with a V6 Mercedes engine. The S216HDS, a three-axle through-deck coach has also been offered in the UK.

Setra offer a much wider range of products in their home market with nine basic 200-series models available in 27 advertised varieties, as shown in the accompanying table. The company also produces rigid and articulated single-deck buses capable of carrying up to 170 passengers.

Setra's German range

	Optimal				Universal				length (mm)
S208	–	–	–	–	HM	–	–	HMU	7,600
S209	–	–	–	–	HM	–	–	HMU	8,500
S211	H	–	–	–	HM	HU	–	HMU	9,660
S212	H	–	–	–	HM	HU	–	HMU	10,370
S213	H	–	–	–	HM	HU	–	HMU	11,290
S214	–	HD	–	–	–	–	HDU	–	11,540
S215	H	HD	HDS	–	HM	HU	HDU	HMU	12,000
S216	–	–	DT	–	–	–	–	–	12,000

Codes
H	low height, rear door
HD	high, centre door
HDS	three axles, centre door
DT	three axles, double-deck
HM	low height, centre door
HU	Universal, low height, rear door
HDU	Universal, high, centre door
HMU	Universal, low height, centre door

Note: the door locations refer to the second passenger door
The Optimal and Universal have different heating and ventilation systems.

Smit

Dutch-built Smit bodies have been available in Britain since 1982. High and low-floor versions are available with all the usual features — direct glazing, a choice of seating and interior trim and a stretched main body side panel. Sales have been fairly low and have been restricted to DAF chassis.

Below:
This is the Smit Euro-Hi-Liner on a rear-engined DAF SB operated by Soul of Olney. The rearmost row of seats is raised above the engine. *G. R. Mills*

675 PBM

Right:
Spot the difference. The Sworder Volvo B10M has a standard-height Alizée body but with a deep windscreen and a low driving position. The British Car Parks Scania K112 has a high-floor body (note the position of the rubbing-strip above the wheel arches) and a normal driving position. The Thorn of Rayleigh Acron integral combines both features — high-floor bodywork and a low driving position.
G. R. Mills (2); SJB

Unicar

Unicar of Spain, whose bodywork was last imported to Britain in the late 1970s, was scheduled to reappear in Britain in 1986 with sales being handled by Ensign Bus.

Van Rooijen

Van Rooijen is an old-established company operating from modern premises at Mont-foort, Holland and building a range of bodies including vans. The distinctive 12m-long Odysee, available in Britain since 1983, was unveiled in 1981. Few have been sold in Britain.

Van Hool

Van Hool is a comparative newcomer to the business of bus and coach bodybuilding — the first bus body was built in 1947 — but it is now one of the biggest builders in Europe. Van Hool's main factory is in Koningshooikt, Belgium, but it also has a subsidiary in Spain.

The extent of Van Hool's presence in Britain has varied over the years although the company has been marketing coaches continuously since the early 1970s. The current T8 range was introduced in 1979 and is one of the most versatile available. The basic Alizée body is normally sold in Britain on 12m-long chassis but shorter versions, down to 8.6m, are available. The Alizée can also be built as an integral with a MAN engine and ZF gearbox. In the UK the Van Hool integral range comprises the Alicron (12m long, low driving position), the high-floor Acron, the twin-deck Astron and the three-axle double-deck Astromega. The Astromega body has been built on Volvo's three-axle B10MT chassis too, although the twin-deck Astral is the normal body for this chassis.

Body sales outnumber integral sales in Britain and the Astromega integral has probably been the least successful of the early 1980s double-deck coach imports. The versatility of the T8 range is illustrated by the supply of bus ('local traffic') versions of the body to Scottish independent Hutchison's of Overtown, while at the other extreme high-

Above:

Van Rooijen's striking Odysee body on a Volvo B10M for Safford of Little Gransden.
G. R. Mills

floor Alizée SH bodies are available on premium coach chassis. Or, to use Van Hool's own words: 'Standardised Van Hool made basic structures are equipped with cozy seating corners, installations for less valid passengers (invalid is what the company really means — Eds), serveries and other comfort items to suit the specific requirements and wishes of each operator.'

The Van Hool range is much more extensive than the T8-series bodies seen in Britain would suggest and includes the A120 (rigid) and AG280 (articulated) citybuses; the novel side-engined AU138 midibus (which has been built with right-hand drive for Japan); various rugged bodies for operation outside Europe; wide-bodied airside buses; and, first shown in 1985, the A280 11.6m-long citybus which offers a low flat floor, a side-mounted engine behind the front axle, and a streamlined frontal profile. Van Hool has also built double-deck bus bodies for service in the Middle East.

The size of the company's output can be judged by the size of recent orders claimed by Van Hool: 500 for Algeria, 550 for Lagos, 100 for Angola and 85 articulated vehicles for Tunisia. Van Hool also makes trailers for commercial vehicles.

Lookalikes

Above right, centre and below; far right, top:
The Alexander body of the early 1960s introduced softly rounded outlines, with much use of curved glass at the front end. The Newcastle Corporation example was on a Leyland Atlantean. Operators specified similar bodies from other builders, including Weymann, as on the BOAC Atlantean, and Roe, for Leeds again on Atlantean; the windscreen did not always sit happily on other body styles. The same screens were even fitted to Northern Counties bodies, as illustrated here on an Atlantean for Ashton Corporation, seen after passing into SELNEC ownership. *SJB collection; Leyland; T. W. Moore; GB*

The most recent example of bodies built to another builder's design also involves Alexander. The R-type double-deck body appeared in 1980, and has been built on several chassis, including Leyland Olympian (*below*), for Strathclyde PTE. South Yorkshire PTE has a large fleet of Dennis Dominators with this body style, and, no doubt in the interests of standardisation, asked East Lancs to build similar vehicles. The Leicester City Bus (*left*), is an East Lancs-bodied Dominator, intended for South Yorkshire, and diverted in exchange for a coach. *SJB; R. L. Wilson*

Right and below:

The family resemblances can cause recognition problems between Leyland's Olympian and Titan models with in-house bodies. The body style originally developed for the integral Titan (*top*), with deep lower-deck windows, was adapted for the Olympian with ECW body; a London Olympian (*centre*) illustrates the similarity. Normal-height bodies on Olympian for NBC fleets were built by Roe at Leeds, and although the main body appears almost identical to the ECW version, the use of Park Royal, rather than BET, screens alters the appearance of this Bristol example (*bottom*). Other ECW and Roe Olympians have been built with deeper, flat screens. *R. L. Wilson; SJB; A. Moyes*

Do-it-Yourself

In the early days of bus operation some operators built their own bodywork. Indeed, two of Britain's best-known present-day bus body builders, Alexander and Eastern Coach Works, started off as body shops owned by bus operators. Nevertheless, most operators chose to patronise specialist suppliers of purpose-built bodywork and the last big operator to fall in line was Midland Red, which built its own bus bodies until 1970. Midland Red had barely ceased body production when the newly-formed National Bus Co linked up with the British Leyland Motor Corporation to build a bus in a jointly-owned factory in Workington: the Leyland National. This association widened and ultimately NBC and Leyland were joint owners of Park Royal,

Roe and ECW too, although this link between operator and bodybuilder was finally severed in 1982 when Leyland acquired NBC's share in the jointly-owned (but Leyland-managed) businesses.

Now the only major connection between an operator and a bodybuilder is at Northern Counties, in which the Greater Manchester Passenger Transport Executive has a major stake. However, on the fringes a number of NBC subsidiaries — such as PMT and Midland Red's Carlyle Works — are becoming involved in the supply of bodywork as minibus converters: in the case of Carlyle Works, a far cry from building D9 double-deckers, but worthwhile business nonetheless.

Above:
Scotland's biggest bus operator, Alexander, established a body-building factory at Stirling to cater for its expanding fleet and to supply sister companies in the SMT group. When the bus company was nationalised in 1949, the coachbuilding part remained independent. This Leyland Tiger TS8 with 39-seat body was built for the Alexander fleet in 1940.
SJB collection

Right:
Midland Red built its own bus bodies (and chassis) at Carlyle Works. Among the more unusual vehicles were a pair of integral underfloor-engined double-deckers, the D10 type. This, the second, was new in 1961 and originally had two doors and two staircases. This view shows it after the rear door and staircase were removed. The body frame was supplied by Metal Sections of Oldbury. *IAL*

Below right:
In 1958-59 Cumberland Motor Services fitted new bodywork to 10 Leyland Tiger PS1s which were 10 years old. Built in the company's workshops, these were among the last half-cab single-deck bodies to be built in Britain. *SJB collection*

Below:
Glasgow Corporation had a long history of tram building and also assembled bus bodies in its Coplawhill body shop until 1962. This Leyland Royal Tiger Worldmaster built in 1956 had a Corporation body on framework supplied by Weymann. It was one of 30. *Harry Hay*

Above:

Liverpool Corporation also did some bus bodybuilding at its Edge Lane works, finishing frames supplied by Crossley and Metro-Cammell. This AEC Regent V was one of 30 similar buses completed by the Corporation over a two-year period up to the end of 1959. They were the last vehicles to be assembled at Edge Lane. Metro-Cammell supplied the framing, and the body was unusual in that it was effectively a four-bay version of Metro-Cammell's Orion, normally built as a five-bay body. *A. D. Broughall*

Below:

Among the independents which have built bus bodies are A & C McLennan of Spittalfield, Perthshire. This Leyland Royal Tiger has McLennan-built bodywork and entered service in 1952. McLennan ceased body building in the early 1960s and withdrew from bus operation in 1985. *SJB*

Who was Who?

The law of supply and demand seems to apply with uncanny certainty to bus and coach bodybuilders. In 1950, at the end of the postwar buying and rebodying spree, there were 78 British bus and coach bodybuilders and these are listed by Alan Townsin in his TPC book *A Wind of Change*. Exactly half were newcomers to the bus business since 1945, and disappeared as quickly. Some were very much in the minor league, with restricted output often for highly localised customers — long-forgotten names like Cumberland Coachwork, Junction Motor Bodybuilding, Lee Motor Body Works and Tower Coachworks. Although most dis-

appeared soon afterwards, some turned to van and truck bodies. Others on the list were major builders in 1950, but would disappear in the next decade: Brush, Crossley, Leyland, Saunders. Of the 1960 survivors, just 20 builders, the next two decades would see many casualties.

First to go was **Burlingham**, an important coach and bus builder, based in Blackpool. The firm's stylish bodies were successful from the start, attracting customers from all parts of Britain, though inevitably many were in northern England and Scotland. Burlingham's most fondly-remembered body was the metal-framed Seagull coach of 1950, a design that lasted, with alterations that were not always improvements, until 1959. Barely had the replacement Seagull Sixty range appeared when it was announced that Duple had acquired control of Burlingham, and the Blackpool factory continued produc-

Below:
Burlingham is best remembered for the Seagull coach body, here on Leyland Royal Tiger chassis for Stark's of Dunbar. *GB*

tion as Duple (Northern). The last 'Burlingham' bodies were built in 1961, and although a separate Blackpool-built range was offered, by 1970 Duple had uprooted from its Hendon, London, base and transferred all production to its present home in Blackpool.

The demise of Burlingham, taken with the demise of **Harrington** in 1965, robbed Britain of two great coachbuilders, leaving the domestic luxury coach body market in the hands of Duple and Plaxton. The Harrington story dates back to 1897, the company initially building bodies for horse-drawn vehicles, then early motor cars, and then commercial vehicles, including early charabancs. Based first in Brighton, then from 1930 in Hove, Harrington built bus and coach bodies for a variety of operators, many based in the southeast. Harrington's greatest hour came with the Cavalier coach body in 1959, a crisp design that found favour with a wide range of operators, including BET group fleets. The last Harrington body, the Legionnaire, anticipated later styles with its square-cut lines, but the firm closed in 1965.

By the time the **Weymann's** factory closed at Addlestone, Surrey, in 1965, the firm had become an integral part of the Metropolitan-Cammell Weymann organisation. Weymann's had started as builders of luxury car

bodies, but progressed to coach bodies in the 1920s. In 1932, with the Birmingham-based Metropolitan-Cammell Carriage, Wagon & Finance Co, it formed Metropolitan-Cammell Weymann Ltd, a sales organisation for the products of the two companies. For some time the products from Addlestone and Birmingham remained clearly different, but latterly the differences were less obvious. Addlestone was used to build the more specialised MCW bodies, including coaches and trolleybuses.

Massey was one of the two major body-builders based at Wigan, though it never achieved the success of neighbour Northern Counties. The first bus bodies were built in the mid-1920s, and Massey specialised in service bus bodies for a group of regular customers, but the company was sold in 1967 to rivals Northern Counties, which used the Massey factory at Pemberton as an extension to its Wigan Lane premises; for a time, the Massey works were used for body com-

Below:
The Harrington Cavalier body was popular with BET group companies. Ribble bought the 11m long version on Leyland Leopard chassis. *GB*

pletion, but gradually all production was transferred there.

The next major closure was not until 1974 when **Seddon** ceased bus body production. Few chassis builders have also built bodies, but in 1947, when Seddon built its first passenger vehicle, it also built the bodywork. Small numbers of Seddon bodies were built, and from 1958 bodies were built on other chassis. A separate company, Pennine Coachcraft Ltd, was set up in an effort to attract more business, and examples appeared in major fleets on Seddon and other makes of chassis. The name reverted to Seddon in 1970, but body production ceased in 1974.

The most notable casualty among the bodybuilders was **Park Royal**, once a major influence on the industry. Formed in 1924 as Hall, Lewis & Co Ltd, the company was succeeded by Park Royal Coachworks Ltd in 1930, based in north London. Park Royal quickly built up an impressive list of customers at home and abroad, most importantly London Transport. In 1946 Park Royal Vehicles Ltd (PRV) was set up and in 1947 acquired Charles H. Roe Ltd, the Leeds bodybuilder. In 1949 Park Royal and Roe were bought by Associated Commercial Vehicles, the group consisting of AEC, Crossley and Maudslay. In the postwar years PRV concentrated on large orders for major customers, including substantial contracts for London Transport. ACV's 1962 merger with Leyland brought a change in ownership, and Park Royal was involved in the 1965 share exchange that brought Bristol and Eastern Coach Works products back on the open market. As a result of its close ties with Leyland, PRV was used for assembly of the sophisticated Titan integral double-decker, but labour problems at Park Royal caused severe production delays, and forced the closure of the coachworks in 1980. Production of the Titan continued at Workington, while other PRV-style bodies were built by Roe at Leeds.

Roe was the next coachbuilder to disappear, a consequence of the decline in the bus body market. Charles H. Roe started building bus bodies at Leeds in 1921, gaining a reputation for well-built composite bodies which sold throughout Britain but most obviously in its native Yorkshire. Roe concentrated on service bus bodies, though coach bodies were built from time to time, and the company's output sold principally to municipal and independent operators. Ownership passed to Park Royal in 1947, to ACV in 1949 and to Leyland in 1962. Although bodies which were recognisably Roe products continued to be built for many years, they gradually came to resemble PRV production, Latterly Roe was involved in assembly of the Leyland Royal Tiger Doyen integral coach, but this created difficulties in a traditional coachbuilder. Roe was closed in 1984, leaving Leyland's bus body production concentrated on ECW at Lowestoft and, to a lesser degree, the Workington assembly plant. The Roe coachworks survived, however, and today houses the Optare firm, which has re-employed many former Roe staff.

Burlingham — a contemporary picture

A 1934 article in *SMT Magazine* described the Burlingham coachworks at Blackpool where, coincidentally of course, a batch of SMT Leyland Tigers was being built. These extracts give some idea of the work of the coachbuilder over half a century ago, and of the language of the time!

'Gleaming fittings and woodwork, mirrors, soft cushions and carpets. These spell the luxury that the world and his wife enjoy, as they range the country in the modern motor coach. Elegant giants of the road, purring as they eat up the miles, they are a far cry from the motor charabancs of yesterday, with their noisy engines, their box-like bodies, and strictly Spartan accommodation for passengers inside!

'The history of their development is a romance in itself. It has added new lustre to the old and honoured profession of coachbuilding. What a debt, for example, the travelling public owes to the famous firm of motor-coach bodybuilders, Messrs H. V. Burlingham, Ltd, whose seaside home is at Blackpool. Their name stands for artistry of craftsmanship — an undeviating quality. Year by year their designers have added new beauty to the motorcoach. Refinements of paintwork and panelling, and increasing ease of interior, are the result of their creative vision . . . Today, in two great works, one in Preston New Road and the other in Vicarage Lane, six hundred busy craftsmen are at work, building anything up to two hundred motorcoach bodies-de-luxe a year. At rush times they are capable of turning out three motorcoach bodies a day. It is an education

Above:
Many MCW single-deck buses were built by Weymann, including 100 Leyland Tiger Cubs with stressed-skin bodies for Edinburgh Corporation.
GB

Above left:
Massey was noted for its curvaceous double-deck body designs, like this Eastern National example on Guy Arab IV chassis, acquired with the business of Moore of Kelvedon.
G. R. Mills

Left:
Seddon-built bodywork only became familiar in Britain in the 1960s and early 1970s. The neat Seddon Midi, on Pennine IV chassis, first carried this style of body, as seen on an Edinburgh Corporation example. *GB*

to visit such works as these and to watch the progress of a coach or bus body from its birth as a gaunt skeleton of wood or metal to its final glory of paint and polish and smooth-sprung comfort . . .

'. . . Now we visit the constructional shop, a vast high-roofed room which resounds with the clatter of power-hammers and other metal-fashioning machinery. These are set at one end of the great shop; at the other you will pause to stare fascinated at the long lines of coach bodies, some nothing more so far than bare frameworks of wood or aluminium, that are being erected inside jigs. Strange creatures they look, too, in their early stages! It is hard to realise that one day soon they will be carrying loads of passengers along the sunlit roads.

'Aluminium panels are being moulded into graceful curves under the deadly beat of the power-hammers. The dexterity of the workers in charge is amazing. To watch them change flat metal into huge rounded panels which will cover the entire back of a coach is to watch a modern miracle.

'Other workers, whose heads are swathed in cloths and whose eyes are protected with goggles, are oxy-acetylene welding, and others are making seat frames and various metal fitments for the coach interiors.

'Panels and fittings, many of them daintily ornamented to give greater grace to the body, pass to the framework in its jig, and are bolted and screwed into place. Floorboards are laid inside; walnut panels hide the ribs of the frame from sight; and other operations follow in rapid succession. Presently, bolted to its own motor coach chassis, it is ready for cellulose paint spraying, for trimming and finishing — the last stages in its transformation from a grub to a gaily-hued butterfly . . .

'. . . Two men, each operating a "gun", can spray a full-sized body in rather less than an hour. Spray, rub-down, and spray again — that is the procedure until the coach has received a priming coat and eight or nine coats of cellulose colour . . .

'. . . But a word about the latest advance in coach body construction. This is the all-metal body, which Burlinghams have invented and patented after some years of intensive research and experiment. It comprises, in a few words, the replacement of the wood body framework with interchangeable sections of aluminium alloy, tremendously strong and utterly rigid. It has been tested over ploughed fields and subjected to many other endurance trials with perfect success. In appearance it differs little from the ordinary wood-framed body, but to the passenger it offers almost complete immunity from fire risks, for there is nothing much to burn in the body, and greater safety in any accident on the road. No shock, it is claimed, can buckle it, concertina, or rip it open, so enormous is its innate strength.

'It offers the motorcoach owner a lighter body with a consequent lessening of fuel and tyre costs. Its sectional construction, too, permits replacements to be made, when necessary, in an incredibly short space of time. Burlingham believe that it is the coach construction of the future. Already all-metal coaches are making their appearance on the roads in increasing numbers . . .

'. . . So it goes on; and presently, a new giant coach, or a new single or double-decker bus, sets out to add fresh grace and distinction to the roads. Spare a thought, next time you climb aboard one, to the artists and craftsmen whose work has made travelling a luxurious and pleasant adventure.'

Burlingham was certainly a pioneer in metal-framed bodywork, though others might question the company's claim to have invented it. The use of aluminium alloy, jigs for body construction, and spray painting indicates how advanced Burlingham was, and many operators mourned its 1960 sale to Duple. The Vicarage Lane works survives as part of Hestair Duple's main Blackpool plant.

Trend-Setting

Bus Trends

The bus industry is not the slave of fashion. Change can be slow, and is often dictated by legal and political considerations rather than by the needs of operators or passengers.

For many years double-deck bodies were predictable — they had 56 seats, 30 up and 26 down, with a rear open platform. Then operators agitated for more seats, and builders obliged by squeezing them in, within the weight and seat-pitch regulations of the time; the highest capacity in 8.23m (27ft) double-deckers was 66 (37/29), but by the time these were built, larger buses were legalised.

With 9.14m (30ft) double-deckers came a fresh interest in forward entrances on front-engined buses. This was not a new idea, but was popular in the period from 1958 to the late 1960s. It was argued quite reason-ably that safety was improved as the doors were under the supervision of the driver, but the resulting layouts were sometimes cramped and less satisfactory than on their unfashionable rear-entrance counterparts. One influencing factor may have been the new rear-engined double-deckers with their front entrances.

At the same time as operators moved towards forward entrances, some operators, notably East Kent, Ribble and Southdown, specified fully-enclosed front end designs — perhaps in an attempt to match the 'modern' rear-engined designs. With the arrival of the rear-engined chassis, double-deck design settled down to another predictable layout; front entrance, rearward-ascending stair-case, and a maximum of 78 seats (44/34). The bodies remained box-like and clearly derived from earlier designs, until inspired use of

curved glass and glassfibre helped improve appearances, and bodybuilders tackled the awkward bustle caused by the engine compartment by fitting engine fairings for a smoother outline. Then came a move to longer windows; Alexander built bodies from the mid-1960s with double-length windows, nearly 2.44m (8ft) long, and, while other builders produced similar bodies, windows settled down at an in-between length of 1.62m (5ft 4in).

Double-deck one-man operation heralded a brief trend towards two-door double-deckers in many of Britain's main towns and cities; but while some, notably London, Lothian and Nottingham, have stuck with the separate entrance/exit layout, most reverted to one-door buses. A more lasting trend was the fitting of forward-ascending staircases, an infinitely safer layout.

There was another brief flurry of interest in longer double-deckers, up to 10m (32ft 10in) long, but this was short-lived. The municipal fleets at Bradford, Leeds, Liverpool, Manchester and Sheffield all tried the longer buses, but most of the PTEs that succeeded them standardised on more manageable 9.5m (31ft 2in) buses. Newcastle's successor, Tyneside PTE, moved on to longer buses, as did

Lothian Region, the Edinburgh municipal fleet; but they were unusual, and buses around 9.5-9.6m are considerably more common.

Single-deck bus development went through similar phases. In the 1950s the underfloor-engined bus with a 9.14m (30ft) body normally had a single front entrance and 44

Far left below:

The forward-entrance layout on front-engined double-deckers was briefly popular until the rear-engined designs took over. This AEC Regent V for Yorkshire Woollen had lightweight MCW Orion bodywork with jacknife doors, a design that was hardly helped by the all-red livery. *AEC*

Below:

One of the operators attempting to project a more modern image with fully-fronted double-deckers was independent Barton Transport. This AEC Regent V with Northern Counties bodywork was unusual in combining a forward entrance with lowbridge seating layout. The use of curved glass screens at the front was also rare on front-engined chassis. A one-piece sliding door was fitted. *AEC*

Above:
Early body designs on rear-engined chassis were fairly bland; the early MCW bodies on Leyland Atlantean were similar to this Great Yarmouth Corporation example.
Alan Millar

Above right:
The first panoramic-windowed double-decker was built by Alexander for Edinburgh Corporation on a Leyland Atlantean chassis in 1965. The windows on the lower deck offside were out of sequence because of the stairwell panel. Note the faired-in engine compartment. *GB*

Right:
Typical of various trends — peaked domes, separate entrance and exit, 10m overall length — a Bradford Corporation Alexander-bodied Daimler Fleetline.
T. W. Moore

The bodywork on London Transport's prototype Red Arrow buses was built by Strachans, the Hamble-based company that enjoyed a brief period of success in the 1960s. The wide doorways featured jacknife doors, the front entrance leading to turnstiles, and the central exit doors were positioned ahead of the seating area. *AEC*

or 45 seats. When 11m (36ft 1in) buses became legal in 1961, many operators simply went for longer buses with extra seats, up to 53, while curved screens, glassfibre and long windows helped to change the appearance. The spread of rear-engined single-deckers in the 1960s prompted experiments with two-door buses (even a solitary three-door bus in Edinburgh), and with seating layouts; many of these buses were built as an alternative to double-deckers, so high passenger capacity was of importance. One way to achieve this was the standee single-decker, with large areas for standing passengers. London Transport's Red Arrow AEC Merlins had seats for 25 behind the centre exit, and a large open space for 48 standees ahead of this; in this way double-deck capacity could be attained, but few operators — and perhaps fewer passengers — liked the standee layout.

The adaptable layout Leyland National of the 1970s allowed operators a certain amount of freedom to specify the number of doors, and the seating layout, but no room to influence the external appearance, other than with their liveries. Not all operators chose Nationals, and some, notably Scottish Bus Group fleets, stuck with the single-door all-seated layout on underfloor-engined chassis; in this way they achieved 53 seats and a nominal 24 standing.

There has always been a limited market for smaller-length buses. Some were needed for rural services, and there have been brief flurries of interest in mid-size buses for urban operation, but none has really been significant enough to warrant the term 'trend'.

A more definite recent trend is the proliferation of minibuses in Britain, normally conversions from van models — although these are strictly outside the scope of this book. The bodybuilders involved in the conversion work have little scope for influencing body layout, and have so far done little with the external appearance. Most remain unashamedly van-like with only liveries to relieve the tedium.

Right:
**Inside a Red Arrow,
showing the turnstiles
leading to the spacious
standing area; the 25 seats
were on a raised area at the
rear, above the rear axle and
engine.** *London Transport*

Below right:
**Many of the present breed of
minibuses are simply
conversions of panel vans,
which present few
opportunities for stylish
looks. Midland Fox's red
and yellow livery for its Fox
Cubs helps to disguise the
lines.** *M. Fowler*

Far right:
**A line of contemporary
coaches at the 1957 British
Coach Rally. Mostly Duple-
bodied, they are a mixture of
lighter-weight Bedfords and
Commers and heavier-
weight AEC Reliances.** *IAL*

Coach Trends

By their very nature, coaches are more
susceptible to fashion than mundane service
buses. In the same way that carbuilders
facelift models every few years, coachbuilders cannot afford regular major restyling and choose to make minor cosmetic
'improvements' for each new season. For a
while coachbuilders seemed to lag behind
their private car counterparts: just as cars
were abandoning chrome and over-
ornamentation, coaches were discovering
them. And the absence of real competition led
to complacency.

Coach bodies were more of a bespoke
product in the 1960s. They were built using
largely traditional methods, still often
wooden-framed, and the principal builders
had visually different ranges for different
chassis. Bodies for the popular Bedford and
Ford lighter-weight chassis were the best-
sellers, while for the heavier-weight AECs
and Leylands, bodies were often to a different
design with, perhaps, a family resemblance.

Panoramic windows and straight-waisted
bodies were the most significant design
legacies of the 1950s. Curved glass side
windows came from the 1960s, as did a move
towards rationalising coach body ranges.
Now all coaches from the smallest midi-size
to the full-length 12m vehicle belonged to the
same range, and were outwardly similar
with the advantages of common parts.

Salvador Caetano bodies which first arrived
from Portugal in the late 1960s provided
British operators with the first taste of
Continental competition, and although these

A bizarre 1950s design that never became a
trend — the half-deck coach, patented by
Crellin-Duplex and built by Mann Egerton.

The staggered twin-deck arrangement allowed
up to 50 seats when most coaches could
accommodate only 41; this AEC Regal IV was
for Ripponden & District.   *IAL*

Right:
Another high-deck design, known as the observation coach, was built by Whitson of West Drayton on Foden PVRF6 chassis in 1952. The raised rear saloon, more reminiscent of airport coaches, allowed additional luggage space. The Foden chassis was unusual: the two-stroke engine was rear-mounted, at least a decade ahead of other rear-engined single-deck chassis. *IAL*

Below right:
The Plaxtons body shop at Scarborough in the late 1950s, with Consort bodies being built on Bedford SB and AEC Reliance chassis. *Plaxtons*

Below:
Ahead of its time? The 12m Alexander M type coach on Bristol REMH chassis was a high-floor, small-windowed, rear-engined design first seen in 1968. This is the Eastern Scottish prototype, in black and yellow livery. *SJB*

Above:
**Exotic coaches like this have become
increasingly familiar. This twin-deck Van Hool
Astral body, on Volvo B10M chassis, was for
Harris of Armadale.** *Van Hool*

offered no real threat to the Duple/Plaxton
establishment, they were chosen by operators
seeking a coach that looked different.

The bodybuilders throughout mainland
Europe were competing for a sizeable
market, and were moving towards crisper,
cleaner lines; they were also experimenting
with body layout. High-floor coaches provided additional underfloor luggage space
for longer-distance services and tours, and in
Britain Plaxton produced the Viewmaster in
1977, a high-floor version of the Supreme.
This was the first British-built high-floor
body to catch the imagination of operators,
although Scottish Bus Group had in 1968
developed the M type body with Alexander for
its Scotland-London express services; this
had a specification that anticipated later
trends — rear engine (on Bristol REMH),
high-floor, small double-glazed windows,
reclining seats, and toilet accommodation.
When SBG required replacements for some of
these vehicles in 1980, Duple produced a
small-windowed version of its Dominant
design, and these coincided with a move back
to smaller-size windows, partly a response to
fashion, partly a reflection of increasing
European concern about coach safety and
strength in a roll-over accident.

With the growing number of imported
continental bodies, squarer — almost anony-
mous — designs were apparently sought by
operators, and Duple and Plaxton were under
pressure to replace their tired-looking
ranges; they responded with new bodies in
1982. The ranges included high-floor
designs from the outset, and these
represented a good proportion of orders.

Belgian builder Jonckheere produced
designs that blurred the distinction between
single-deck and double-deck coaches. Some
had low-slung rear passenger saloons,
behind the rear axle and reached by an
internal staircase; others had low driving
positions, allowing clear forward vision for
passengers, some builders even carrying the
passenger saloon forward above the driver.

In parallel, double-deck coaches were
becoming more popular. British operators
had flirted with these over many years, but
without widespread acceptance. One of the
consequences of the 1980 deregulation of
express coach services was the appearance of
the German-built Neoplan Skyliner double-
deck coach in service with British operators,
and other European builders have exported
similar models to Britain. Domestic manufacturers have produced competing models,
notably the integral Metroliner from MCW,
and body designs from Alexander, East
Lancs and Eastern Coach Works — although
apart from the Metroliner all have been
somewhat less luxurious than the imports.

Further consequences of the 1980 Act were
the increasing number of integral coaches on
the road, and a trend towards rear-engined
coaches. Although engine position hardly
affects the look of modern coaches, it can
influence layout; double-deck coaches are
normally built on rear-engined chassis, while

coaches with rear saloons can only be built on mid-engined chassis. The Plaxton 4000 body illustrates some of the options. In full double-deck form it is built on the rear-engined Neoplan N722 underframe; in RS form, with rear saloon, it is built on Volvo's underfloor-engined B10MT chassis; in MS form, with mid-mounted lower saloon, it is built on the Scania K112TR rear-engined chassis.

The demand for better coaches has helped to improve specification. Double-glazing, bonded windows, tinted glass, soft-trim interiors, reclining seats, galley compartments and toilet/washroom accommodation, all facilities that were rare in the 1970s, have become accepted as the norm on many coaches today.

Above and top:
Rear-engined integral coaches allow builders to provide large amounts of underfloor luggage space. The Leyland Royal Tiger Doyen demonstrates the easy access provided for luggage, electrical components, wheels and the engine. Leyland demonstrated the luggage capacity of the Doyen by fitting 100 suitcases into the locker space. *Leyland*

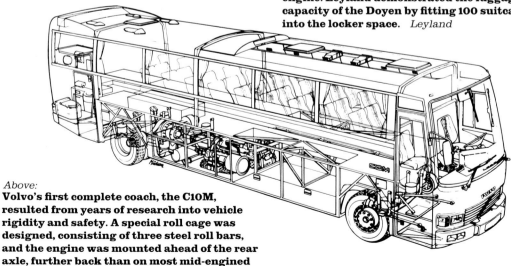

Above:
Volvo's first complete coach, the C10M, resulted from years of research into vehicle rigidity and safety. A special roll cage was designed, consisting of three steel roll bars, and the engine was mounted ahead of the rear axle, further back than on most mid-engined designs, for stability through weight distribution. *Volvo*

Dedicated Followers of Fashion

Above, overleaf and page 104:
Although currently fashionable, double-deck coaches are not new. The impressive Guy with Strachans body was built in 1929 for service between London and Manchester. The Ribble 'White Ladies' were Leyland Titans with fully-fronted bodywork, in this case a 1948 Titan PD1/3 with Burlingham body. Ribble's next family of double-deck coaches were the 'Gay Hostesses', Leyland Atlanteans with MCW bodywork supplied for use on early motorway services. They used basic bus body shells with coach fittings and external trim. Another generation of Ribble group coaches is represented by the 36ft Standerwick Bristol VRLL, built in 1968, with ECW bodywork — in many ways anticipating the style that is currently popular. Neoplan reintroduced the double-deck coach concept to Britain with the Skyliner model, here in Yelloway ownership.

This was followed by the Van Hool integral Astromega model, shown here in Titterington Holidays livery, a more crisply-styled coach in the Van Hool tradition. British builders then produced double-deck coaches based on existing models; first was the Leyland/ECW Olympian, as built for NBC fleets, using existing body framework. The Maidstone & District Invictaway coach is typical of these. For the 1984 Motor Show Leyland produced a restyled version of this vehicle, in Ebdon's livery; in this form it has a family resemblance to other current Leyland coach models — and the windscreen was first seen on Manchester's 1968 Mancunian bodies. MCW took its three-axle model for Hong Kong as a basis for the Metroliner, a vehicle that has been built for NBC and SBG fleets, and Tyne & Wear PTE.
IAL(2); Michael Dryhurst; ECW; R. L. Wilson; Van Hool; Leyland (2); MCW

Standardisation

In theory there is much to be said for standardisation. Increased production of a single, or similar, product should reduce costs for the builder and the customer, and hence for the passenger. Operators with sizeable vehicle requirements are able to lay down standards and expect builders to meet them, but of course smaller operators have less muscle. The alternative is that manufacturers impose the standards, but some operators are unhappy about this loss of freedom. We have already looked at the influence that operators can have on the design of buses and coaches (see the chapter on Operator Influence), and we have seen that bodybuilders are apparently not always ready to accommodate them.

Probably the first attempt at standard-isation was the Milnes-Daimler double-decker of 1904, followed quickly by the London General B type, which more than 75 years ago was built on a remarkably sophisticated production-line system. The principle of mass-producing identical buses made great sense for the vast General fleet, enabling easier storage of spare and replacement parts, and quicker overhaul by staff familiar with the model. London has largely stuck to the concept since, benefiting particularly from its World War 2 experience in aircraft production; this was reflected in

Below:
The London General B type was the first real standardised bus produced in quantity. *IAL*

Right:
London Transport's postwar standard was the famous RT type, with jig-built bodywork allowing a high degree of interchangeability. *GB*

Below right:
The Tilling group's standardisation policy meant that near-identical buses could be found in many parts of the country, right down to liveries and destination layouts. This is a 1951 Eastern Counties Bristol KS5G with Eastern Coach Works body. *GB*

Below:
London Transport accepted standard 'off-the-peg' models for its late 1970s/early 1980s deliveries of Leyland Titans and MCW Metrobuses, and preferred to stick to the Mk 1 version of the Metrobus, with its distinctive asymmetrical windscreen. *SJB*

the jig-built interchangeability of the post-war RT family, and allowed London Transport to concentrate its bus overhauls on Aldenham and Chiswick, facilities designed around a highly-standardised fleet.

With RTs and Routemasters the system worked excellently; the buses were designed so that the body and mechanical components could be separated at overhaul, and as overhaul times differed, bodies were almost inevitably rematched with different chassis; a 'float' of extra bodies was always maintained to keep the system moving. With newer types, London Transport found that these would not fit into the Aldenham programme, leading to reports of dissatisfaction with 'off-the-peg' buses, and premature disposal.

Outside London, the greatest degree of standardisation was achieved by the Tilling group, with, in the 1950s and 1960s, a very simple range of models built at its in-house Bristol and ECW factories. During this period there were usually at any one time three models — a single-deck, double-deck and rural single-deck model. With Tilling fleets taking nothing else, there were economies of scale, and with the ECW bodies there were standardised panels, windows, ventilators, seats, moquettes and a whole range of fittings; therefore there were fewer parts in store and staff were familiar with the product. Even the paint store was kept simple, for most Tilling buses were either red or green. Compare this situation with the

operators — usually municipal — buying different chassis/body combinations each time because of the need to accept the lowest tender. It certainly makes sense for the ratepayer, and adds variety for the enthusiast — but pity the poor engineer!

Since 1970 there has been a move towards greater standardisation. The Leyland National was the most obvious example, but with integrals like the Metro-Scania, Metropolitan, Metrobus and Titan, operators have accepted a more standardised product. Not that all choice has been removed; one can usually specify the number of doors, the number of seats, seat-covering, provision of luggage space, number and type of ventilators, destination layout, and many minor features.

Coaches have become much more standardised. At one time there could be a very different body style for each chassis, but such luxuries are not practical now. With their 1970s ranges, Duple and Plaxton produced

Below:
Although models like the Metrobus, here in Mk 2 form, are highly standardised, operators can change specifications to suit local circumstances. This Reading Transport Metrobus has coach seats and forced ventilation (hence the lack of opening windows) for its Goldline express service to London. *Ian M. Train*

Above left and left:
Standardisation throughout Plaxton's Paramount range means that all sizes of coach have components in common. Although at different ends of the scale, the little Bedford YMP-S of Kemp of Clacton-on-Sea is clearly related to the Newton's of Dingwall Paramount 4000RS on Volvo B10MT chassis.
G. R. Mills; John Burnett

Below left and above:
The Alexander Y type body enjoyed a long production run, and was built in bus, coach and dual-purpose form on a wide variety of chassis, front, mid and rear-engined. A 1963 Alexander Midland Tiger Cub coach contrasts with a 1982 Eastern Scottish Seddon Pennine VII bus. *GB; SJB*

variations on the same body style for everything from midi-coaches to high-floor 12m coaches. These achieved commonisation of parts to protect investment in new windscreens, domes, roof sections, etc.

Standardisation also implies a long production life for bodies. Where once body designs were changed frequently, it is now common for ranges to have a long 'shelf life'. Many of the designs from Continental builders — Jonckheere, Mercedes-Benz, Neoplan, Setra, Van Hool — have all been long-running, with minor improvements. Plaxton's Paramount of 1982 looks set for a long life, and has spawned a whole range of variants. Duple's range has changed twice since 1982, but for political as much as for commercial considerations.

Service bus bodies are less susceptible to fashion, and stay on the market for many years. The '1970s standard' body, still offered by Northern Counties, looks perfectly acceptable today, and has allowed Greater Manchester Buses to build up a highly-standardised fleet; the Alexander Y type body, in production for 22 years, did much the same for Scottish Bus Group fleets. And there have been other bodies that have lasted, virtually unchanged, for long periods.

Not a Pretty Sight

While designers no doubt intend all bus and coach bodies to look good, by common consent they do not always turn out that way. Here are some notable uglies.

Below:
Bellhouse Hartwell built some amazing coach bodies around 1950, including this 37-seat Foden for Greatrex Tours, with some strange features. *Don Morris*

Below left:
Always admired for its body designs, Burlingham rarely got it wrong. The company did, though, with this 1959 variation of the Seagull on front-engined chassis, a most unhappy combination of shapes at the front end. The coach is a Bedford SB in the colours of Stark's of Dunbar. *GB*

Right:
Fishwick of Leyland operated this Leyland Atlantean with bodywork by its associated company, Fowlers. *SJB*

Right:
Willowbrook was called on to build some normal-height bodies on Bristol VRT for NBC fleets in the 1970s, devising a style that used the pillar spacing of other contemporary bodies, and an ECW-like front panel, but without the subtlety of the originals. *SJB*

Top:
This Ipswich East Lancs-bodied Leyland Olympian has a basically sound body style spoilt by the odd detailing at the front end — the fussy headlight arrangement, single leaf front door and the extra window behind this.
G. R. Mills

Above:
CIE's new-generation bus family, built by Bombardier and GAC, would win no prizes for styling. The high degree of common parts means that single-deck examples can look functional and attractive, but the double-deck model is an uneasy-looking confection.
R. L. Wilson

Making the Best Impression

Once upon a time, bus and coach liveries often looked as if they had been designed by the general manager's wife on the back of an envelope. Sometimes they were. Or they were municipal liveries, unchanged in colour and application over decades, irrespective of vehicle design.

Indeed, vehicle design may have provided the original influence; many colour schemes owed their layout to the body mouldings on the Leyland Titan TD1, for example, and operators continued to apply them to all bodies, irrespective of design. Even coach bodies tended to dictate liveries, with their distinctive flashes and mouldings, which gave operators limited scope for individuality.

Interest in liveries was reawakened in the 1970s. National Bus Company discarded a sometimes distinguished selection of traditional liveries in favour of depressingly corporate poppy red or leaf green; the new PTEs had introduced new liveries, notably SELNEC's orange and white; the reorganisation of local government prompted municipal fleets to adopt new liveries; and improved coach body designs with smoother sides encouraged more appropriate and adventurous colour schemes.

Now the situation is much healthier. Coach bodies allow scope for free expression, and service buses, so long conservative, even boring, have blossomed into a whole range of new schemes. Trend-setting liveries that break away from the essentially horizontal lines of most bus designs include Midland Fox, Badgerline, Kelvin Scottish and Brighton & Hove. With the formation of municipal bus companies and the approaching privatisation of NBC companies, more new liveries can be expected.

As liveries become more adventurous and operators move away from traditional concepts, the need for professional advice on colours, layout and typography has been recognised. Larger companies often have in-house designers, while others use consul-

tants like Ray Stenning, whose work is becoming familiar in many parts of Britain.

Ray Stenning will be known to many as a writer and photographer, contributing to *Buses* and the trade press, and to *Buses Annual*. Often these have covered aspects of vehicle and livery design, and he has had the chance to put his theories into practice. His liveries include designs for Bakers of Weston-super-Mare, Oxford City's Nipper minibus, Green Line's Speedlink coaches, the United Counties 1986 bus livery, the London Country and Luton & District minibuses and the Oxford Citylink Metroliner double-deck coaches; the Metroliner livery won the 1985 Livery of the Year competition in *Commercial Motor*. We asked Ray Stenning about his livery work.

Can you tell us something about the brief for the Bakers coach livery?

'This was a fairly open brief; initially they wanted a new livery — modern, striking, yet not cheap, and preferably based on blue, perhaps incorporating green. It was for a new Jonckheere P90 to be used exclusively on their new daily London service. Bakers gave me a fairly free hand, and the final livery was my own development of my initial concept, taking the client's wishes into account.'

Did you find it different working for an NBC subsidiary like Oxford?

'With the Citylink livery there were some constraints; existing colours and the NBC coach house-style — which I call the venetian-blind effect. But I chose to interpret these to better effect, to make the livery simpler and more dramatic. I set out to create an eye-catching, striking effect in harmony with the lines of the Metroliner, and at the same time advertise the essential nature of the service. So I kept the graphics in tune with the existing style, but made them tougher, tighter, more immediate — to become part of the overall impact of the

Above:
Recognisably in the same family as other NBC 'venetian-blind' liveries, Stenning's design for the Oxford Citylink Metroliners made a few subtle changes to good effect. The predominant colours are blue and yellow, on a white base. The lettering is in proportion to the size of the vehicle. *Ray Stenning*

livery, rather than simply applied as an afterthought.'

And what about the Speedlink livery?
'Yes — quite a few constraints on this one! For a start the livery had to reflect the up-market nature of the Heathrow-Gatwick Speedlink service, not a great problem; but it also had somehow to be identified with NBC, British Airways and British Caledonian, the partners in the venture. Not an easy task!'

How did you tackle this?
'My interpretation meant effectively that it had to have the NBC "venetian-blind", blue (for BA and B Cal), yellow for B Cal and red for BA. I also wanted to include white and grey, for B Cal and BA respectively. I devised the livery to incorporate these colours in a way that would turn heads and would suggest air travel, up-market business air travel at that. There is a hint of BA's "speedflash" in the "venetian-blind", which helps achieve this, as do the colours themselves. I also wanted to eliminate the "tip-toe" look of the high-floor Berkhof body, and did

this mainly with the broad yellow band to bring the eye down, the use of blue right down the skirt, and the thin white at the immediate under-window level.'

Were you responsible for the Speedlink namestyle?
'Yes, I designed the namestyle and graphics. Originally I wanted to see it white (SPEED) and grey (LINK), with auxiliary lettering in lemon yellow. There were client plans to change the lettering to all-yellow, but we reached a compromise on all-white with yellow lettering. This livery demonstrates better than most that it is not just a matter of putting pretty colours on to a coach; it is really a visual interpretation of many facets — a single identity of a multiple function. Incidentally, the worst constraint of the Speedlink job was having less than 24 hours to do it in!'

Do minibuses present particular problems?
'Definitely. The uncompromising shape of the bodywork can cause difficulties.'

Do you prefer to have a totally free hand?
'Ideally, but in practice this is not always the case. It can be challenging to work within constraints, but the client should not be too rigid. It is essential to define the purpose of the livery, which is based on the vehicle type and use, the firm's standing in the marketplace, the firm's image of itself — and the public's image of the firm.'

*Are you frustrated by coach body details —
mouldings, grilles, hinges, etc? Would you
prefer close liaison with bodybuilders?*

'Yes to both questions! Rubbing strips always
seem to be in the wrong place — some
apparently identical bodies even have rubbing strips at different heights along the
bodyside. Yes, I would certainly welcome
much closer liaison with the bodybuilders.'

*Should liveries be continued into vehicle
interior?*

'In essence yes, but not slavishly. There are
some attractive moquettes offered by bodybuilders, and some nasty ones, so it shouldn't
be too difficult. At the very least an interior
scheme should be sympathetic to the
exterior.'

*Do you believe that a livery is a livery is a
livery, to be applied in standard form to all
types of vehicle, or should liveries adapt to
different body designs?*

Liveries must adapt to each vehicle, and
should be adapted by the designer, not the
customer! I adapted the Bakers livery in this
way, though the layman wouldn't notice, and
shouldn't notice because the overall effect has
remained constant.'

Has a livery a 'shelf-life'?

'Hard to answer this one. Familiarity must
not lead to contempt, yet liveries don't
continually need to change. Obviously if the
purpose of a particular livery changes, it
becomes inappropriate.'

*Should operators be influenced by fashion in
livery design — flashes, stripes, strong
colours, bold fleetnames?*

'Again, hard to answer. As you might expect,
I feel that operators should be influenced by
professional designers! What this means is
that to achieve an overall effect, a livery
might incorporate some "fashionable"
element — but only if this is totally
appropriate.'

*Lastly, and maybe unfairly, what about
current liveries generally? And any specific
likes and dislikes?*

'There are a few good liveries about, but sadly
many abysmal ones. There are stripes
dodging about all over the place, unco-
ordinated, unrelated shapes, silly wedges,
terrible graphics with hideous unreadable
typefaces; you should have a licence even to
look in a Letraset catalogue! Likes? Well —
London Buses, Flightline (the Green Line
version on its Berkhofs), Merseyside PTE,
Greater Manchester PTE, and a few others.
Dislikes? Well . . . Southdown's Stage-
coaches, National Express, Badgerline and
Bristol Cityline, and many more! Especially
anything with *Euro* in its name, or *Executive*, or *Cruiser*, or *Hiliner* — and worst of all
Euro-Executive Hiliner Cruiser! Oh yes —
and any coach with a complete inventory of
its internal fittings on the back window in
white Letrasign!'

Coats of Many Colours

Operators' attitudes to liveries have changed. The low-cost approach which gained ground in the 1960s led to simplification, usually triggered off by the adoption of spray painting which was seen as being more cost-effective than traditional brush painting. Now more operators are adopting not only new liveries, but new livery layouts, many of which are breaking away from the traditional layers of colour. The Eastern Coach Works body as fitted to the Leyland Olympian has been chosen to illustrate the effects of different livery layouts because it is a vehicle which can be seen in most parts of Britain and which probably wears a greater variety of liveries than any other standard double-deck bus.

Right and below:
Liveries can alter the appearance of identically-bodied vehicles, as these contrasts illustrate. This Alexander RL type body on MCW Metrobus underframe, as originally supplied to Midland Scottish, is in the traditional azure blue and cream livery (*top*). With the formation of Kelvin Scottish in 1985, a new livery was devised, using a pale blue colour with azure blue relief (*centre*). The Kelvin livery variation adopted later in 1985 is also shown (*facing page, top*), with the azure blue limited to the skirt behind the front wheels and an angled stripe. *SJB(3)*

Facing page, bottom:
The simplest livery layout, apart from the overall application of one unrelieved colour, is to divide the body by a band of light-coloured relief; the fast-disappearing NBC corporate livery is of this type. Eastern National, the owner of this bus, adopted a bright colour scheme of yellow and green in 1986.
G. R. Mills

Above:
The application of broad layers of colour is a traditional way of breaking up the bulk of a double-deck bus body. Lothian Region Transport also uses traditional municipal colours, maroon and white. Having a dark colour at the bottom helps minimise the effect of road dirt on the appearance of the bus.
Ian N. Train

Below:
East Midland's dual-purpose livery on this Olympian uses the same basic layout of colours as the Lothian bus in the accompanying picture, but with the addition of contrasting stripes of relief which look disjointed and give a somewhat fussy appearance to the bus. The stripes, angled back as they reach higher up the side of the body, pick up an NBC corporate theme. *A. R. Kaye*

Above:
Midland Red North picks up the same theme of angled stripes on this vehicle in Midland Express livery of white with red and yellow relief. The effect is striking. *SJB*

Below:
Clever use of colour (predominantly blue and white, relieved with green and yellow) and shapes that disguise the fundamental boxiness of the Van Hool Astromega distinguish Ray Stenning's livery for Bakers of Weston-super-Mare.

Rebodying

Chassis over the years have tended to last longer than bodies and there have always been a few operators who have chosen to have ageing chassis reconditioned and fitted with new bodywork as an alternative to buying a complete new bus. This practice was at its peak in the early-1950s as poor-quality wartime bodies deteriorated while the chassis to which they were fitted still had a reasonable life expectancy. But it became much less common in the 1960s and 1970s, initially because old front-engined chassis were generally considered obsolescent and therefore not worth rebodying, and latterly because the Government's grant towards the purchase of new buses made a complete

vehicle a more attractive buy than a body for an existing chassis. Rebodied vehicles did not attract the Government grant. Rebodying became restricted to accident-damaged vehicles whose original bodies were beyond economic repair.

The 1980s have seen the discontinuation of the Government's new bus grant and a small number of operators have chosen to rebody 15-year old chassis: the Chester, Cleveland and Southend municipal fleets have all recently had bus chassis rebodied. Southend has also had some Leopard coach chassis fitted with new engines too, effectively giving the company many of the benefits of a new coach for something over half the price.

Above:
A rare example of fitting a new body to a light-duty chassis is illustrated by this 1980

Bedford YNT in the fleet of Head of Luton. It has a 1985 Plaxton Paramount 3200 Mk II body. *G. R. Mills*

Above:
East Kent had new Berkhof bodies fitted to 10 AEC Reliances in 1984. These vehicles dated from 1973 and originally had Duple bodies, but new 'A' prefix registrations gave them the appearance of new coaches. *SJB*

Below:
This Midland Red (South) coach with 'Q' prefix registration is a 1976 Leyland Leopard PSU3 which was rebodied by Plaxtons in 1984. Its original body, also by Plaxtons, had been damaged by fire. *SJB*

Body Language

Air conditioning A method of providing chilled air to the interior of a vehicle. Common in hot climes, rare in Britain. Also very expensive to install.

Auxiliary heater An oil-fired heating system which works independently of the conventional hot water circulation system. Some types can be pre-set to switch on while the vehicle is unattended so passengers do not turn up to board a cold coach. Often known by the trade names of the main manufacturers, Eberspacher and Webasto.

Bay The space between two structural pillars.

BET windscreen Double-curvature screen developed by the British Electric Traction group in the early 1960s for fitment to single-deckers. Became standard on NBC buses and is still in use by ECW for bodies on Olympians.

Bonded glazing See direct glazing.

Bristol dome On coaches, a roof-mounted destination display or illuminated fleetname panel. So called because it was developed for fitment to bodies mounted on Bristol coach chassis with front-mounted radiators which precluded the provision of a destination display below the windscreen.

Bus grant doors Used to describe power-operated doors (usually glider type) on coaches which are designed for use on regular bus services. The name is derived from the new bus grant paid by the Government in the 1970s towards the cost of vehicles meeting certain criteria including a minimum doorway width of 2ft 11in (89cm). Also known as express doors.

Cantrail A structural member which runs the length of the vehicle between the windows and the roof.

CKD Completely knocked down, applied to bodywork shipped from one country to another in the form of a kit for local assembly in the country of destination.

Continental door An entrance/exit on the offside of the body to allow passengers to board or alight on the pavement-side of the vehicle when it is being used in countries which drive on the right. Also known as a continental step.

Above:
The BET windscreen on a Southdown ECW-bodied Bristol VRT. *SJB*

Top right:
Plaxtons' Bristol dome on a Ford in the fleet of Excelsior of Bournemouth. *SJB*

Centre right:
Bus grant/express doors on a Duple Laser body on a Tiger owned by Delaine of Bourne.
G. R. Mills

Bottom right:
A Jonckheere-bodied Scania of Len Wright Travel with a continental door ahead of the rear axle. *SJB*

Cove panel Curved panel between body side and roof.

Demountable body Common on trucks but not on buses. A body which can easily be removed from the chassis and replaced by another body, perhaps of a different type.

Direct glazing A method of glazing whereby windows are glued directly to the body structure instead of being held in place by rubber mountings. Also known as bonded glazing.

Double-decker A bus or coach with two passenger saloons, one above the other.

Double glazing The use of two sheets of glass with a small gap between them to improve body insulation. An increasingly common fitment to high-specification coaches of the 1980s.

Express doors See bus grant doors.

Fixed windows Windows which cannot be opened, as on most modern coaches.

Forced-air ventilation The provision (usually on coaches with fixed windows) of individual passenger-controlled ventilation nozzles on the underside of the luggage racks. Not to be confused with air conditioning.

Glider door Generally a two-piece door in which the panels swing apart as the door opens.

Half-drop windows Opening windows which are lowered vertically and were last used on British bodies in the mid-1950s. Also quarter-drop, as on London Transport Routemasters.

Highbridge A conventional double-deck bus with a central gangway on both decks flanked by rows of pairs of seats. Buses of this type are typically around 14ft 6in (4.42m) high. (See also lowheight.)

Hopper vent A section in the top of the windows of a bus which is hinged at its lower edge and can be pulled open from the top to provide ventilation.

Integral A vehicle in which there is no separate self-supporting chassis and in which the body provides structural strength. In practice there are various degrees of structural integration, blurring the once fairly clear distinction between vehicles with chassis and those without.

Jacknife doors A two-piece door which is vertically hinged and folds together as it opens. May be a single jacknife or a double jacknife with a pair of doors as, for example, on the Leyland National.

Facing page, top:
The only demountable PSV body in Britain is in service on the Isle of Arran. A van body can be fitted to this small Dodge — the join is visible where the window line changes. *SJB*

Above:
A glider door on a Duple Dominant bus body fitted to a Trimdon Motor Services Leyland Tiger. *Leyland*

Above left:
Half-drop windows on a Weymann-bodied Leyland Titan PD2 in the Portsmouth fleet.
A. D. Broughall

Left:
A hopper vent (on the first lower deck side window) and top-sliders on a London Buses MCW Metrobus II.
S. J. Butler

Above:
A lowheight body — able to squeeze under a 13ft 6in bridge. *Leyland*

Lowheight A double-deck bus with conventional centre gangway on both decks but based on a low-framed chassis, thus reducing the overall height by up to 1ft (30.5cm) when compared with a highbridge bus.

Lowbridge Used to describe an obsolete style of double-decker with a sunken side gangway on the upper saloon and rows of four-passenger bench seats. This layout reduced the overall height of the double-deck bus by about 1ft (30.5cm). The last lowbridge body was built in 1968.

Normal height (Of a double-decker.) See highbridge.

Parallel action doors Used principally on rear-engined coaches to give access to the luggage area in the wheelbase. Doors of this type are not hinged but pull clear of the body and lift upwards while staying vertical and parallel to the body sides. They require less

space to open than do conventional hinged doors which describe a wide arc as they swing out from the body; they are therefore advantageous for coaches which are likely to have luggage loaded or unloaded in confined spaces such as a busy coach station.

Plug door A single-piece outward-opening door which remains parallel to the body side as it swings out and back to open — like a parallel-action luggage door but operating in a different plane. Commonly used on modern coaches. Allegedly provides a better seal when shut, thus reducing draughts and wind noise.

Through-decker A high-floor coach with seating above the driver's compartment.

Top-slider A section at the top of a bus window which can slide open to provide ventilation. There are also half-depth and full-depth sliders for use in tropical climates.

Twin-decker A high-floor coach with a passenger compartment located behind the rear axle and below the main saloon floor (eg Jonckheere P90, Plaxton Paramount 4000RS).

Above left:
Double-jacknife doors on a Wadham Stringer-bodied Bedford YMQ-S of Eastern National. *S. J. Butler*

Left:
A plug door swings clear of the body: this is an Alexander TC with direct glazing. *SJB*

Below:
Coach bodies are sometimes used as the basis for other specialised vehicles, like this Leyland Tiger with Duple Caribbean bodywork for the National Blood Transfusion Service, known, rather disconcertingly, as the 'Bloodmobile'. *Duple*

Coach interiors have changed greatly over the past 35 years. The Scottish Omnibuses coach in the first photo, a 1953 Alexander-bodied AEC Regal IV chassis, has seating of a modern style, but the rest of the interior, from the moquette on the seats to the veneered wood on the ceiling, belongs to the 1930s. The roof quarter-lights were a popular feature of the time. The Bebb coach, on Bedford VAM, dates from the 1960s, and shows the move to deeper, longer windows, still with sliding ventilators, but a greater use of plastic for roof and side facings. The seats are fashionably low-backed, non-recliners, with a bright moquette. Typical of modern coaches is the Van Hool body on Leyland Tiger, with soft trim and carpeting, curtains and blinds, fixed windows with forced-air ventilation, and discreet lighting. The seats are recliners.
Alexander; Duple; CIE